About Demos

Demos is a greenhouse for new ideas which can improve the quality of our lives. As an independent think tank, our aim is to create an open resource of knowledge and learning.

There are no easy solutions to society's problems, and we should be bold in imagining alternative futures. We can start by recognising the potential for people to change their own lives through self-government.

Demos connects researchers, thinkers and practitioners to an international network of people changing politics. Our ideas regularly influence government policy, but we also work with companies, NGOs, colleges and professional bodies.

Demos knowledge is organised around five themes, which combined to create new perspectives. The themes are democracy, learning, enterprise, quality of life and global change.

We also understand that thinking by itself is not enough. Good ideas grow out of practice. Demos has helped to initiate a number of practical projects which are delivering real social benefit through the redesign of public services.

www.demos.co.uk

First published in 2003
© Demos
All rights reserved

ISBN 1 84180 105 4
Typeset by Land & Unwin, Bugbrooke
Cover design by Peter MacLeod, macleod@theplanningdesk.com
Printed by Printflow

For further information and
subscription details please contact:

Demos
The Mezzanine
Elizabeth House
39 York Road
London SE1 7NQ

telephone: 020 7401 5330
email: mail@demos.co.uk
web: www.demos.co.uk

Beyond Measure

why educational assessment is failing the test

Paul Skidmore

DEM☉S

Contents

Acknowledgements

I am grateful to the Edexcel Foundation for supporting this research. Particular thanks to Frank Wingate, Steve Besley and Stevie Pattison-Dick for their contribution throughout the research process. Thanks also to Neal Lawson, Craig Leviton and Hugh Simpson at LLM.

In the course of the research, I have been grateful for the scholarship of Professor David Hargreaves, Professor Paul Black and Professor Dylan Wiliam, all of whom were kind enough to offer some specific comments and advice on the ideas in this pamphlet. Thanks also to Mike Tomlinson and Dr Ann Hodgson for sharing their thoughts and experience, and for all those who contributed to the Demos/Edexcel symposium on the future of educational assessment (see Appendix 1).

I would like to thank colleagues at Demos past and present for their support, especially Matthew Horne, Will Cavendish, Cath Jones, Jake Chapman, Rachel Jupp, John Craig and Greg Lowden. Eddie Gibb and Peter Macleod masterminded the production process with customary aplomb. Finally, thanks to Tom Bentley for his invaluable advice at every stage.

Needless to say, any omissions or errors remain my own.

Paul Skidmore
February 2003

Glossary and abbreviations

A2	–	the second half of the new, 6-unit A-level structure (under Curriculum 2000)
AfL	–	Assessment for Learning
AQA	–	Assessment and Qualifications Alliance
AS	–	Advanced Subsidiary, first half of the new 6-unit A-level structure (under Curriculum 2000)
GCSE	–	General Certificate of Secondary Education
GNVQ	–	General National Vocational Qualification
GTC	–	General Teaching Council
ICT	–	Information and Communication Technology
JCGQ	–	Joint Council for General Qualifications
NCC	–	National Curriculum Council
NCSL	–	National College for School Leadership
NCT	–	National Curriculum Test
NCVQ	–	National Council for Vocational Qualifications
OCR	–	Oxford, Cambridge and RSA Examination Boards
OECD	–	Organisation for Economic Co-operation and Development
PISA	–	Programme for International Student Assessment
PSHE	–	Personal, Social and Health Education
QCA	–	Qualifications and Curriculum Authority
SAT	–	Standard Assessment Task
SCAA	–	School Curriculum and Assessment Authority
SEAC	–	School Examination and Assessment Council
TGAT	–	Task Group on Assessment and Testing
TQA	–	Teaching Quality Assessment
TTA	–	Teacher Training Agency
VCE	–	Vocational Certificate of Education

1. Introduction

Since we cannot know what knowledge will be needed in the future, it is senseless to try and teach it in advance. Instead we should try to turn out people who love learning so much and learn so well that they will be able to learn whatever needs to be learned.

John Holt

This report seeks to clarify an agenda for addressing the major challenges and opportunities facing the assessment and qualifications system over the next decade.

It has been written during a period in which the debate about assessment for certification, and public scrutiny of the actors that deliver it, has reached an unprecedented intensity. Yet the clarity and depth of this debate has not improved, though it is now being conducted at a higher pitch. This has followed a series of increasingly high-profile operational failures on the part of the exam boards and the Qualifications and Curriculum Authority (QCA), and fears of full-scale system meltdown in autumn 2002 amid accusations that thousands of A-level students had wrongly had their results downgraded. That the true scale of the problem subsequently turned out to be much less serious than was first reported serves only to underline the current fragility of the assessment and qualifications system, and the ease with which it can be thrown into crisis.

The government's response to these problems, and its intention to reform both qualifications and the systems of educational provision that underpin them, have in some respects been constructive and novel. Alongside a series of measures designed to restore confidence in marking and grading, it has laid out an ambitious reform agenda, particularly for 14–19 education.

The essence of the reform programme is the desire to combine increased diversity and flexibility of provision with increased transparency and seamlessness in credit, award and entitlement.

Thus, in establishing targets for improving both the quality and provision and participation in education post-14, the government has also indicated its desire to create a single, unified award framework over the long term. This objective is partly intended to address and correct a historic weakness in British education – the separation between vocational and academic education and the traditionally poorer deal that young people pursuing vocational options have experienced. It is also in part designed to anticipate and meet the challenges of ongoing change in the wider landscape of learning – the need for higher levels of knowledge and skill, problem-solving ability and new expectations in the world of employment.

Significantly, the government has not sought to produce a detailed blueprint for the structures that will emerge, or the ways in which they should be implemented. This may be the result of necessity – the systems that need to be reshaped are both complex and stubborn.

But it also reflects a growing understanding of the impossibility of comprehensive, top-down reform based on 'objective' knowledge about what should occur and how. The idea that government could determine in full detail everything that should happen in such a system is not credible, and growing numbers of ministers are prepared to acknowledge this.

So what principles of reform and implementation should be used as an alternative?

This pamphlet sets out an alternative agenda, based on what we believe is a compelling vision for learning and the way it can be served by educational qualifications and assessment.

The myth of omniscience – the idea that government can know all it needs to in order to create and deliver the best possible outcomes for a system as complex as education – carries strong echoes of the assumptions and principles that underpin educational assessment and qualifications themselves. The recent controversies over the A-level have revealed deep-seated and largely backward-looking beliefs about the kind of functions that different forms of assessment can be expected to perform. Government has begun to acknowledge that the *quantity* of formal testing now undertaken, the cumulative effect of almost a generation of reform, may be having a negative effect on learners and teachers. But the debate about the *quality* and purpose of assessment remains half-hidden in expert briefings and academic disputes. It is time it was brought centre-stage.

Our argument is that, while genuine knowledge and understanding remain as vitally important as they have ever been in education, our understanding of what assessment represents and how it should be used needs to change fundamentally.

It would be possible to restructure the formal qualifications and award framework radically, while at the same time doing little to adjust or improve the underlying mode or methods of assessment on which awards rest. This would be a missed opportunity of epic proportions, and would further deepen the logistical and organisational problems already besetting the examinations system.

Instead, we travel in the opposite direction – asking what it would be necessary to change in the dominant model of educational assessment that could give the current reform agenda – and those policies that might come after it – the greatest impact on the knowledge, understanding and learning ability of young people and wider society.

The pamphlet is grounded in the recent issues and conflicts that have dogged the assessment system, and it begins to think about how we might identify and address the underlying causes of system failure. However, it takes as its starting point the view that this kind of reactive, operational focus does not acknowledge the fundamental challenge the system faces.

The current set of reforms has combined a determination to restore the credibility of the system in the short term with a longer-term focus on the creation of a unified award framework for the whole of the 14–19 phase. The danger is that while their rhetoric and rationale are future-focused, the reforms will end up looking backwards into history for the models and assumptions on which to build a new approach.

In order to counteract this risk, we need to address important questions about the actual purposes we want assessment to serve, and how it needs to be reshaped to accommodate the social, economic and technological changes implied by the transition to an information society. The Labour government's reaction to the A-level dispute in 2002 has created a great opportunity for a deeper and further-reaching examination of the purposes and assumptions underlying the assessment and qualifications systems. But this opportunity must be taken seriously. It is all too easy for debate to focus on a set of short-term considerations, including re-establishing stability in the existing system, without tackling bigger issues that remain just out of view. The speed with which the International Baccalaureate has been taken up by some as an instant panacea for the problems of the A-level is symptomatic of the myopia of the current debate. Time and again, it deteriorates into an unhelpful argument about the design and relative merits of different award frameworks, without engaging in the much more important prior conversation about precisely what it is we should be assessing, how we should assess it, and why.

Central among the system's current problems is that we have allowed too many functions to be assigned to the system without considering the implications for its capacity to perform them effectively. To change the qualifications structure might restore credibility in the short term, but by failing to address the assessment system's underlying problems the respite would only be temporary, and might well come at the expense of its long-term vitality.

In this report, we make the case for the progressive transformation of both assessment *and* qualifications, based on a new shared vision of what we actually want them to do.

A new vision

At the core of this new vision, we believe, should be a very simple proposition: that assessment is, first and foremost, about *making learners better learners.* The great irony of our current system is that our school qualifications do not really 'qualify' us to do anything, at least not in the way that achieving a certain standard of competence can qualify us to drive a car or fly an aeroplane. In most cases, all that school-level qualifications really qualify us to do is some more formal learning. An A-level in biology, for example, is not sufficient to become a veterinary surgeon or a general practitioner, but it does provide necessary proof of an ability to learn the requisite skills and competencies if given the opportunity to do so. Few employers really expect potential employees to have all the skills they need to perform their role successfully, but they are looking for evidence that a new recruit will be able to learn what they need on the job.

The question we have to ask is whether our current approach to assessment is really designed to improve people's ability to learn, and whether our current system of qualifications is really configured to make the inferences we draw about this ability to learn as valid as possible.

Some may interpret this line of argument as an attempt to dismiss 'knowledge' and 'content' from the qualifications debate, and even from the function of education itself. This is misguided. The form of assessment for learning that we advocate in this pamphlet is grounded in the need for *greater* command of knowledge and *deeper* forms of understanding. It does not seek to downgrade the forms of rigour or academic excellence that some traditional qualifications have helped to attain. But it questions the extent to which a model tied to particular forms of decontextualised assessment can remain insulated from rapidly changing circumstances, and argues that a qualifications system focused on knowledge *and* the ability to learn can serve the needs of students, education institutions, employers and the rest of the society in more robust and more responsive ways. A system that is genuinely fit-for-purpose, we will argue, can and should be structured through a different set of principles.

The reason why this is so important is rooted in the changing role of knowledge in the structure of economic and social relations. Learning, however and wherever it took place, has mattered throughout human history because 'no one is born with the ability to function competently as an adult in society'.[1] Over the centuries, what constituted an 'ability to function competently' has evolved to reflect the changing demands and expectations of particular societies and their prevailing systems of social and economic order. The simultaneous growth of specialised and technical knowledge has only added to the importance of the systems we use to verify and certify this ability. But whether they were used for placing people within the mass production systems of the industrial economy, or for certifying an apprentice's competence within the craft system of the pre-industrial economy, or for unlocking access to university education, traditional forms of assessment were predicated on the assumption that the range of skills or competences citizens or workers would need to demonstrate was narrow and durable.

That assumption is now increasingly suspect. In recent decades we have witnessed an information technology revolution and the emergence of an economy that is globally integrated and increasingly 'informational', in that 'the productivity and competitiveness of units or agents in this economy (be it firms, regions, or nations) fundamentally depend on their capacity to generate, process and apply efficiently knowledge-based information'.[2]

Over the last generation we have also seen massive change in educational participation, and in the uses to which qualifications and assessment results are put. The shift to majority participation in post-compulsory education, and to mass entry into universities, has applied new pressures on the systems of examination used to sort students one from another. The use of assessment information as a central tool for improving standards of performance among schools and students also alters the dynamics acting on the system as a whole, often in unpredictable ways, as we explore in later chapters.

These longer-term shifts render obsolete a model of education or training that expects to teach young people by the age of 21 everything they will need to know for the rest of their life. Our skills, abilities and understanding will need to be refreshed and adjusted continuously throughout our lives. By European Commission estimates, 80 per cent of European Union workers will need significant retraining over the next decade because of the impact of new technologies on their existing work practices.[3] By 2010, 65–70 per cent of employment opportunities will require a Level 3 qualification[4] or higher.[5] The 'half-life'[6] of most workplace skills is now just three-and-a-half years.[7] Employers consistently report that the skill requirements of most jobs continue to rise steadily. These informational demands also extend beyond the labour market to the domain of citizenship and society. There is a growing recognition that public services cannot continue to deliver solely on behalf of their users without their active engagement in identifying and creating positive outcomes. In health, for example, major improvements will only be realised if citizens take more responsibility for their own well-being, accessing information to diagnose ailments and identify treatments, and finding out how they need to adapt their lifestyle to live a healthier life. Active citizenship, in short, requires active learning.

Of course, most of this learning will not take place in formal educational settings. Instead, provision will be increasingly diverse, flexible and personalised – through distance learning and online technologies, the reorientation of existing educational providers towards smaller, more manageable chunks of 'just-in-time' learning, rising investment in human capital by employers, the emergence of corporate universities, and a more prominent role for local community organisations in provision. But the flip side of personalisation is that individuals will need to become more proactive, self-governing and entrepreneurial in their approach to learning, equipping themselves with the knowledge and skills they need to fulfil their ambitions.

The best gift that formal education can therefore offer our young people and, in turn, the employers and communities that will come to rely on them, is a capacity and a hunger for learning. Assessment is crucial to both. Only by verifying how well what has been learnt has been understood, how confidently it can be drawn on in a range of different contexts, and how effectively it can be applied to solve practical, real-life problems, can we hope to improve our capacity to learn in the future – literally, to learn how to learn. But an assessment system that measures recall of knowledge rather than depth of understanding, that tests only a narrow section of the curriculum, and that demotivates and lowers the self-esteem of learners is not fit for this purpose.

Instead, the principle of *assessment for learning* should become the foundation of a radically reshaped assessment and qualifications system. Assessment for learning is 'any assessment for which the first priority in its design and practice is to serve the purpose of promoting pupils' learning'.[8] Reorganising the system around assessment for learning would enable us, as far as it is possible, to mitigate and in some cases transcend the conflicts that the current arrangements produce. In particular, it would enable us to do six things.

1. By improving and certifying ability to learn as well as knowledge and understanding, it would allow the assessment and qualifications system to be reshaped to serve the key strategic function of school-age education in the twenty-first century.
2. By linking the design and timing of assessment and qualifications to the progress of individual learners, it would allow continued diversification of the range and timing of assessment episodes without placing unbearable strain on the organisation and regulation of assessment.
3. By highlighting the contribution assessment can make to powerful learning, it would embed assessment in the practices of teachers, learners and school without inappropriately defining the parameters of their teaching and learning.
4. By recognising the value of teacher assessment, it would enable assessment for summative purposes to be both more valid and more reliable.
5. By re-emphasising the robustness of assessments carried out in classrooms and schools, it would reduce the logistical complexity of the assessment system and its dependence on an over-stretched, centralised external

marking process, while simultaneously increasing its transparency.

6. By reclaiming assessment for learners, it would better prepare all those that pass through it for a career as a lifelong learner.

A practical agenda for change

Constructing a new vision for assessment and qualifications is only part of the task, however. We also need a clear route map to guide us through difficult organisational and political terrain if radical reform is to be sustainable. There is no quick fix that will instantly satisfy every stakeholder, because the demands that each makes on the system – and the values that underpin them – are very different. For government, the task of leadership is not to try and identify some definitive answer to the system's problems but to create what Ronald Heifetz calls a 'holding environment' in which these conflicts can be reconciled through the negotiation of positions, adjustment of values and adaptation of behaviour among all involved.[9]

The reform process set out by the government in the recent strategy document, *14–19: Opportunity and excellence*, offers a partial outline of a new approach.[10] But it does not contain all the elements needed to succeed in the long term. In particular, it does not establish sufficiently clear connections between the principles and practices of the 14–19 phase and the operation of earlier phases of education; the ways in which other parts of the system create a foundation for better learning later on, and standard frameworks for assessment, award and reward create constraints within which the rest of the system has to operate.

Further, the policies set out in the 14–19 strategy do not explicitly address the roles and capacities that the exam boards – pivotal institutions in the attempt to raise both standards and participation – will need if they are to play a full part in the transition that policy-makers now want to achieve.

We should also shift the focus away from trying to develop qualifications frameworks that are rigidly durable. As we have seen with A-levels, systems that are oriented towards preserving a 'gold standard' are often ill-equipped to reinvent and reconfigure themselves to changing needs and circumstances. In the future, the only durable qualifications frameworks will be those that are capable of *adaptation*. As Schön argues, 'we must become able not only to transform our institutions, in response to changing situations and requirements; we must invent and develop institutions which are "learning systems", that is to say, systems capable of bringing about their own continuing transformation'.[11]

So a realistic agenda for reform must be long term, and take account of the rapidly changing social and economic environment to which the assessment system must adapt if it is to survive in the long run. We outline the five principles of a new approach.

1. Qualifications should qualify you for something, and that something should be further learning.
2. Assessment should combine the best of academic and vocational practices in order to certify not just what you know, or what you can do, but how well you learn.
3. Within a decade, everyone should be entitled to receive a personalised programme of learning that reflects their individual profile as a learner and which should be assessed appropriately.
4. The purpose of assessment in schools should be to generate authentic and formative data about learners and their future needs, and other purposes should not be allowed to predominate.
5. The provision of learning and its validation and certification should not be a closed shop.

This set of principles clearly has profound implications for the way we think about assessment and for the education system more widely. We outline what we believe to be the five most important implications:

o   for teachers' professional development and the organisations that support it

○ for the basic methods used in assessment
○ for employers and their interface with the assessment and qualifications system
○ for the way higher education relates to school assessment
○ for the relationship between assessment data and performance management.

The pamphlet proceeds as follows. Chapter 2 sketches out the context in which the present debate about assessment is taking place, introduces the concept of 'complex adaptive systems' and suggests why this may be a helpful theoretical lens through which to analyse the current problems. Chapter 3 takes this analysis further by considering the question of why, and to whom, qualifications and assessment is so important, emphasising that these multiple and competing perspectives lie at the heart of the system's complexity. Chapter 4 examines some of the additional strains that have been placed on the system in recent years, and the predictable impact these have had on its performance. Chapter 5 sets these changes against the remarkable consistency of the basic methods by which assessment has been delivered over the last 50 years, and questions whether these are still 'fit-for-purpose'. Chapter 6 makes the case for an alternative assessment paradigm, based on recent evidence about how people learn and the potential contribution of assessment for learning to educational outcomes. Drawing on this alternative paradigm, chapter 7 sets out five principles of reform and possible implications (outlined above) and identifies some of the root and branch innovations needed for this agenda for change to be realised. It concludes by acknowledging the fundamentally *political* character of the decisions that need to be taken, but suggests that government has an unprecedented opportunity to take the long-term view that reform of the assessment and qualifications system requires.

2. The context: assessment and qualifications as a complex system

Reform of the assessment and qualifications system looks set to be the single most important educational issue of the next few years. The perennial controversy over the 'dumbing down' of standards is as old as the exams system itself. But after a series of high-profile operational failures on the part of the exam boards, culminating in the A-level marking dispute in summer 2002, the debate about the future of the assessment and qualifications system has developed a life far beyond the media's August silly season.

Partly in response to this imperative, new proposals aim to achieve long-term reform of the systems surrounding award and qualification. But for these objectives to be achieved, the set of pressures and contradictions currently acting on the system need to be resolved.

Three basic paradoxes lie at the heart of the current problems. The picture they help to paint is of a system:

○ that is faced with a countervailing pressure for standardisation amid growing concerns about preserving accountability, reliability and fairness given the logistical complexity of the tasks involved
○ that has been affected by profound changes in the social, political and economic environment that surrounds it, but which still relies on the same basic, paper-and-pencil methods for delivering assessment which have scarcely changed in 100 years

O   that is routinely criticised by learners, parents, politicians, academics, employers and the media, but which has proved extraordinarily resistant to radical change.

Assessment, for both end-of-phase qualifications (GCSE, A-level, NVQs), and National Curriculum Tests (NCTs or 'SATs') used to measure school performance, has acted as a major lever for raising educational standards. But as with other aspects of educational delivery – for example, the recruitment and retention of teachers, initiatives to encourage local innovation or strategies to accelerate improvement in the lowest performing schools – the assessment system has been forced to juggle competing demands, and has found it increasingly difficult to do so.

Providers of assessment services have been pulled in different directions, struggling simultaneously to diversify and to standardise their provision. On the one hand, they have been asked to manage escalating expectations and more diverse patterns of demand and provision. They have been expected to provide greater breadth through a wider choice of subjects and qualifications, and greater flexibility in the way these are delivered in terms of modularisation, a wider range of alternative assessment dates and so on. On the other hand, they have continued to rely on methods and organisational arrangements whose role and scope have expanded far beyond their original place in educational delivery. As the QCA's Chief Executive Dr Ken Boston has put it, the assessment system resembles a 'huge cottage industry'. Yet it has been forced to deliver much higher volumes of assessment and to work to tighter deadlines in an atmosphere of increasing political sensitivity.

The implications of steadily ratcheting up the tension on what was already a taut organisational environment have become ever more visible in recent years.

First, this build-up of pressure has resulted in a proliferating array of unintended consequences that have become more serious in scope, scale and frequency:

Narrowed focus – as the old adage runs, 'what you test is what you teach'. In high-stakes situations, teachers and learners have an obvious incentive to focus on those subjects that are tested (at the expense of achievement in non-tested areas like personal, social and health education) and, within subjects, to concentrate on improving aspects of performance that are likely to be tested at the expense of other dimensions of achievement within the curriculum.[12] In doing so, students can raise their attainment on the test without improving their performance on the ability it is designed to assess.

Cheating – complaints about cheating in NCTs reached record levels in 2002, although cheating is no longer the preserve of students. The threat of a poor league table position or special measures has created an incentive for school leaders to manipulate test scores. One national newspaper identified 26 possible methods of cheating by headteachers, teachers and classroom assistants.[13]

Grade fixing – until recently, it had been assumed that grades were being fixed upwards. Improvements in assessment performance were routinely put down to falling standards with examiners becoming more generous, particularly to borderline candidates, and the cumulative impact being 'grade inflation'. Needless to say, the question of maintaining standards over time is far more complex (see Box 1). However, as the scandal that engulfed the assessment system in summer 2002 illustrated, the facts of the matter are less important than the corrosive effect of the debate itself on the system's performance. The recent scandal was ostensibly about grade 'deflation', with the grades of some students apparently fixed lower than they should have been, precisely so that accusations of grade inflation could be countered.

Box 1 The fallacy of the great 'grade inflation' debate

The publication of GCSE and A-level results now produces an annual public and media outcry about whether improvements in performance are authentic or whether they merely show that the exams have got easier.

In an attempt to deflect traditional criticisms, QCA commissioned an international panel of experts to investigate its procedures for assuring quality and standards over time.[14] It concluded that:

'To answer the question of comparability of standards and to make a legitimate interpretation of trend data over time, certain conditions would need to be met, including that:

O   the specifications and syllabuses have remained constant
O   the examinations given are common over time or can be equated
O   there have been no changes in educational policy or practice intended to raise performance.

None of these conditions have been met as there have been numerous changes to the system' (emphasis added).

In other words, it is almost impossible to ascertain whether exams have got easier over time. It is also rather pointless. For, as syllabuses quite properly change over time to reflect new demands and capabilities, comparisons of relative difficulty almost inevitably come to depend on value judgements about the kinds of skills and aptitudes that are most important.

Second, as these unintended consequences have proliferated, government and regulators have found themselves making greater demands of the system and being drawn into increasingly visible interventions. Even before the Summer 2002 crisis, the government announced that the incoming chief executive of the QCA would have new powers to intervene in the activities of the exam boards, but also that ministers would work much more closely with the QCA and intervene in its activities where necessary.[15]

This increase in executive oversight and control was an understandable response to an ongoing series of increasingly visible system failures. Yet despite (or quite possibly because of) this growing day-to-day involvement, both government and the QCA have struggled to reconcile the tension between restoring short-term stability, and articulating a vision for the longer-term trajectory the system should follow. Creating the kind of regulatory climate in which the organisational and methodological innovation needed to realise this vision might flourish seems even further away.

Third, these interventions have not managed to 'fix' the problems of the assessment system; on the contrary, they seem to have made it more fragile. We have therefore witnessed further interventions and growing evidence of 'regulatory creep' as these interventions produce unintended consequences of their own.[16] Indeed, the interim report of the Tomlinson Inquiry identified this as one of the principal triggers of the Summer 2002 crisis. It concluded that an intervention by the QCA chairman designed to ensure that the 2002 results showed broad continuity with the 2001 results was misinterpreted by the exam boards, leading the OCR board in particular to put inappropriate weight on statistical evidence about the distribution of marks.[17] This subsequently has led to an animated discussion about what the role and institutional position of the QCA should be vis-à-vis government.

Fourth, as the system has lurched from one crisis to another, we have seen rising levels of acrimony with government, the QCA and the exam boards blaming each other for the system's problems. The media have targeted their criticism at all three, although they have singled out ministers (and contributed to the resignation of the Secretary of State). In this atmosphere, it is perhaps unsurprising that we have also seen growing numbers of students seeking legal recourse for decisions by exam boards that, for example, deleteriously affect their chances of going to their preferred university.[18]

The case for a systems approach

As the various stakeholders consider their next move in the aftermath of the 2002 crisis, the emphasis has quite properly been on stabilising the assessment system and trying to prevent a full-scale meltdown. The second phase of the Tomlinson Inquiry included a number of sensible recommendations about organisational and structural reforms to enable next year's examinations to run more smoothly. But the danger is that unless these are accompanied by a radical shift in the way we think about the *nature* of the assessment system, they will amount to little more than rearranging the deckchairs on the *Titanic*.

In particular, we believe that a systems approach is essential in developing reform strategies that can recognise and accommodate the complexity of the assessment and qualifications system. The four problems identified above are entirely predictable modes of failure when an entity like the assessment and qualifications system, which displays the characteristics of a *complex adaptive system,* is subjected to traditional command-and-control assumptions that do not reflect the way the system operates. Specific failures may sometimes be predictable but, even when they are, pre-emptive action will only shift the problem elsewhere by producing unintended consequences of its own. In other words, when a complex system is managed as if it were a machine, the one thing that is predictable is unpredictability. As Chapman argues:[19]

- O   *Unintended consequences become more frequent,* as the system does not respond to change in a linear, predictable fashion.
- O   *Top-level interference increases,* as the operation of the system is distorted and its capacity reduced by the imposition of external demands, and policy-makers blame implementation professionals for failing to change.
- O   *The system becomes more fragile,* as interventions reduce the overall performance of the system and generate new problems that require fixing with further interventions.
- O   *Levels of acrimony and blame rise,* as different agents within the system fail in formulating policies to take account of the different perspectives of other agents on the nature of the problem and its most appropriate solution.

Like all complex systems, successful reform of the assessment and qualifications system (and the wider education system of which it is part) depends on being able to take a holistic overview, and to understand the interconnections between different components of the system. Systems thinking also helps to show how systems of organisation will adapt to radical changes in their external environment without changing their under-lying characteristics. Restructuring and reorganisation on a superficial level can take place without touching a much more fundamental set of values, mindsets and assumptions about 'the way things work'. In this case, it is particularly relevant to note that the basic features of the modern assessment and qualifications system would be recognisable to someone familiar with the system as it looked 50 or even 100 years ago, despite massive changes in the wider context in which it is expected to operate.

Finally, and perhaps most importantly, a recognition of the existence and the validity of different 'frames' or ways of looking at an issue is a central feature of systems thinking and practice. Addressing these *multiple perspectives* is an essential precondition for reshaping the way the assessment and qualifications system works. This is particularly difficult in a situation where the appearance of objectivity seems to be an overriding goal for so many people involved in the system. But preserving the myth that judgements of educational attainment have some kind of external, scientifically verified status as objective truth is unsustainable. While so many stakeholders continue to look for ways of shoring up this mis-perception, the system is unlikely to fulfil its full potential. In reality, giving up on the search for 'the answer' that will fix the system's problems is likely to be the first step towards a more sustainable approach to measuring educational standards – a somewhat ironic conclusion given the status of 'the answer' in our current school and university system.

How these multiple perspectives currently play out is the focus of the next chapter.

3. Why assessment matters

To understand why assessment is so important, we should think about the multiple roles that assessment is now expected to perform. So far in this pamphlet, we have used the term 'assessment and qualifications system' as if it were a single, unitary entity but, as Box 2 illustrates, the information that assessment provides serves several different functions, of which evidence of attainment for individual certification is only one (albeit perhaps the most visible).

Box 2 A typology of assessment?

It is widely accepted that it is a mistake to try and distinguish between different *types* of assessment, because all assessment involves the same basic process: seeing how well a learner is progressing. Instead, it is more helpful to differentiate between the uses served by the information gleaned from assessments. In this sense, assessment can be:

○ *Formative*, so that the positive achievements of a pupil may be recognised and discussed and the appropriate next steps may be planned

○ *Summative*, for the recording of the overall achievement of a pupil in a systematic way

○ *Evaluative*, by means of which some aspects of the work of a

---

school, an LEA or other discrete part of the educational
service can be assessed and/or reported on.

Task Group on Assessment and Testing (TGAT)[20]

TGAT also included *diagnostic assessment*, through which learning
difficulties could be identified and appropriate remedial help
provided, but it acknowledged that the overlaps between
diagnostic and formative assessment were considerable.

To see how these different uses overlap, interact and conflict, we have to
consider *why* assessment matters, and *to whom* it matters. This also helps
to illustrate why it has historically proved so difficult to change this system.

So who are the stakeholders in the assessment system, how do their
perceptions of what assessment is for differ, and what are the key tensions
that this produces? The answers relate to three levels of purpose: learners,
the wider education system, and society in general.

Learners

The central function of assessment is providing learners with information
about their current levels of knowledge and understanding, and to guide
them in making decisions about what they do next. It shapes how they
perceive their comparative strengths and weaknesses across the curriculum
and, on this basis, acts as a guide in choosing between different pathways
and subjects. For teachers, assessment provides essential information about
how they need to adapt their practice to meet the individual needs of their
students, whether in terms of content or teaching style. This assessment is
primarily *formative*.

Assessment is, of course, also used to make decisions *about* learners.
These decisions, often taken very early on in their lives, can profoundly
affect the course they take. This assessment is primarily *summative*.
Sometimes these decisions will be relatively formal. Further and higher
education institutions, for example, depend on the information that
assessment provides to enable them to select students and match them to
appropriate learning opportunities. They are only able to do this if

qualifications (and therefore the assessment processes underpinning them) are seen as valid statements of students' underlying attainment and the breadth and depth of their knowledge across the curriculum areas relevant to possible future programmes of study. In the labour market, moreover, assessment for certification acts as a form of currency used in the process of sorting individuals into occupations and roles, enabling employers to select the most suitable candidates and jobseekers to identify employment opportunities that best suit their skills and experience.

But equally important decisions may be informal. Assessment performance can shape the expectations that teachers have of learners from a very young age (with all which that implies). Perhaps most crucially, assessment performance affects the decisions learners make about themselves and their own self-worth, and for this reason assessment remains for many the most traumatic experience of their education.

The education system

As Hargreaves has argued,[21] assessment comprises one leg of a three-legged stool that shapes educational practices: what is learnt and taught (curriculum), how it is taught (pedagogy) and how this learning is judged (assessment). To a great extent, the frameworks and standards captured in qualifications frameworks define the parameters of what it is possible to teach and how it is possible to learn. Although the specification of curriculum content has played a stronger role in driving change during earlier periods (most obviously during the introduction of the National Curriculum), the centre of gravity in the system has tended to shift back towards assessment. In the UK, this bias has been linked to the central importance of assessment to the standards agenda, which has dominated educational policy-making for more than a decade. The aggregation of assessment data in various ways is seen as the principal means of increasing the transparency and comparability of school performance, and enabling the choices that parents and children make between schools to be a vehicle for driving up standards. This assessment is primarily *evaluative*.

This reinforces the importance of understanding the ways in which curriculum, assessment, pedagogy and learners' own behaviour combine to produce different outcomes. This is the only way to create integrated strategies for 'aligning' the assessment system (see Box 3) with the purposes we want the curriculum to serve. As Biggs argues, 'assessment is almost certainly the most important single component in the system: get assessment wrong and you get everything wrong'.[22]

> ### Box 3 Key concepts: alignment
> 'Alignment' refers to how well the different elements of the education system – assessment, curriculum and pedagogy – work together to promote improved student outcomes. The concept is perhaps best associated with Professor John Biggs, who coined the term 'constructive alignment':
>
> 'Effective teaching in a constructivist [active learning] framework requires that the relevant and appropriate high cognitive level activities that students should display are addressed both by the teaching methods and by the assessment tasks (which in any case become the curriculum to the students). This is "constructively aligned" teaching.' [23]
>
> For more on the concept of alignment, see Biggs or Rothman et al.[24]

Society

Assessment has enormous symbolic power in sending out a message about the skills and competences that society values as important, and provides important components of the systems used by a wide range of institutions to make decisions about people and resources. For government and citizens (or voters), the further aggregation of assessment data provides a marker of progress in the delivery of a key public service and a means for holding political leaders to account for their promises to improve educational standards. It enables the success of schools, colleges and teachers to be evaluated and compared, and policy decisions adjusted accordingly. This assessment is also *evaluative*.

Qualifications and assessment also provide a vocational currency – a way of validating people's knowledge and skills that can be used by employers and other education providers to sort applicants into groups, determine who get access to opportunity, and set pay levels. The school-age qualification system sits at the base of an increasingly complicated set of arrangements for 'validating' people's knowledge in ways that enable the labour market to function more widely, ie university degrees, professional associations and qualifications, and various pay bargaining and reward structures. School-age qualifications still play a hugely important role in sorting young people into different groups and influencing the pathways that they take in later life.

However, as other organisations across society and the economy increasingly merge innovation and learning processes with their everyday organisation, learning takes place in a growing range of settings, through team-based and collaborative processes of enquiry and interaction. If we are not careful, the current qualifications framework, and the need for it to serve aggregative, comparative and performance management roles, may militate against the innovative capacity of community groups, the private sector and other potential providers to deliver learning in a wider range of contexts, and of learners to assess their own strategies and performance.

The role of these parallel institutions in helping to specify, verify and maintain particular standards of outcome achievement in relevant areas of learning is crucial. Moves towards individualisation and modularisation of qualifications frameworks and assessment episodes reflect the growing complexity and diversity of the society surrounding the formal educational process, and the growth of specialist knowledge and specialised forms of learning provision.

Competing demands

In sum, the uses to which assessment information is put include:

- O validating existing knowledge and acting as a passport to further learning opportunities
- O screening for different vocational pathways, broadly corresponding to professional/white collar/trade-specific/ occupational schemes
- O gaining access to some schools
- O informing employers' hiring decisions
- O generating performance information about schools, leading to

differential status and precipitating particular kinds of intervention strategy.

As a result, the list of stakeholders in the assessment system is so expansive as to include almost all of us at any one time in some role or other: learners, parents, teachers, schools, universities, employers, community, voters, government or citizens. But it is also clear that for all these stakeholders the purpose that assessment is expected to serve is slightly different, and in some cases this can lead to competing views on what assessment should look like. Recognising these multiple perspectives on assessment, and acknowledging that each is valid with reference to its particular context and frame, is an important step in understanding the pressures under which the assessment system has to labour and why change driven from the centre is and has been so difficult to achieve. So what would happen if this kind of organisational environment, already creaking under the strain of coping with these divergent expectations, were subjected to a series of new pressures? This question is explored in the next chapter.

4. Strains on the system

We saw in the last chapter that the assessment system faces the inherent difficulty of accommodating and managing the diverging viewpoints of different stakeholders. But this difficulty has been exacerbated by a set of pressures, including both long-term trends and more recent policy and organisational developments, which have contrived to ratchet up the strain on the institutions and practices of assessment to breaking point. They include:

- levels of educational participation
- the volume of assessment
- the restructuring of the qualifications 'market'
- 'free-riding' on the school system
- rising expectations of performance.

Levels of participation

Levels of educational participation and formal achievement, particularly among women, have been rising steadily for the last 25–30 years. The cumulative impact of these trends has been dramatic:

- In 1976, 27% of 16–18-year-olds were in full-time education; by 1990 this had risen to 36%; and at the end of 2001 it was 56%.[25]
- In 1976, around 15% of boys and 13% of girls left school with

at least two A-levels. By 1998, this had risen to 21% and 25%, respectively.[26]

O   Twice as many men and five times as many women went on to enrol on undergraduate courses in 2000/01 compared with 1970/71.[27]

The design of the tripartite phase structure established by the 1944 Education Act, which survives largely intact today, was based on a much more elitist assumption about participation in further and higher education than is prevalent today. In particular, the GCSE/O-level, originally conceived as a terminal qualification for the majority of school-leavers at the end of compulsory schooling, is for most pupils now a rather cumbersome passport to further learning. The green paper, *14–19: Extending opportunities, raising standards*, made clear that government accepts that the current shape of the 14–19 phase is anachronistic. Its medium-term vision is for GCSEs to 'evolve to become a *progress check* around the midpoint of the phase' (emphasis added),[28] with the principal focus being a new overarching award at the end of the phase. The subsequent strategy document, *14–19: Opportunity and excellence*, confirmed this ambition, and announced the intention to introduce 'hybrid GCSEs', mixing academic and vocational provision.[29] But with government committed to a target of 50 per cent of those under 30 entering higher education by 2010,[30] pressure on the assessment and qualifications system to expand post-16 provision still further is likely to grow over the next decade.

Volume of assessment

Higher levels of educational participation are not the sole cause of this expansion in demand for assessment. The actual volume of testing has increased dramatically in the last 15 years, and English children are often described as the most over-examined in the world. The sheer scale and complexity of the assessment system is now difficult to comprehend: simply in terms of assessment for certification, it involves more than a million children, 54,000 examiners and moderators and around 25 million separate test scripts.[31] An average pupil will now take 70 exams by the time they finish school, and with the introduction of world class tests high-achieving students could expect to take as many as 100.[32] As a result, assessment has become a major drain on educational resources: a typical secondary school's exam entry fees have risen from around £50,000 a year to more like £100,000 in the space of three years.[33] The total bill for testing reached £218 million in 2002.[34]

The three principal drivers of this increase have been:

○   the growing centrality of the 'standards agenda' in educational policy-making
○   the desire to diversify and broaden the range of post-16 educational choices
○   the increasingly direct influence for individuals of exam 'passes' to their status, access to opportunity and earning power.

The creation of a National Curriculum in 1988 and the introduction of compulsory assessment for 7, 11 and 14-year-olds were core components of the Conservative government's drive to improve educational standards by increasing the transparency of the school system and making schools more accountable for the performance of their pupils. The insistence that teacher assessment be supplemented[35] by a system of nationally prescribed tests[36] and, later, that these needed to be externally marked, resulted in a step-change in the volume of assessment.

More recently, and more significantly, major reforms to the A-level qualification were introduced under the 'Curriculum 2000' proposals. The existing structure of three subjects studied over two years, which had long been criticised for forcing students to specialise too early,[37] was replaced to enable students to select a more diverse combination of subjects and qualifications via the new, one-year AS levels (which can either stand alone or be upgraded to full A-levels by taking the corresponding A2 units[38]) and the introduction of a new framework for vocational A and AS levels to replace the GNVQ. While the underlying spirit and rationale of the Curriculum 2000 reforms have been welcomed, there have been widespread concerns about the way it has been implemented and the enormous additional burdens this has placed not just on assessment but on the school system more widely.[39] In June 2001, the first year of the new AS award, some 600 AS exams had to be fitted into a three-week period, a logistical and operational nightmare in terms of timetabling, use of school facilities, and staff time. Then in 2002, the first year of the A2, it became clear that the entire assessment system had been so preoccupied with avoiding these logistical challenges that, incredibly, papers were allowed to be set, sat and marked before there was a clearly agreed understanding of how much harder the A2 should be than the AS.[40]

Restructuring of the qualifications 'market'

Alongside and in response to these changes, the recent history of the assessment system has been one of radical restructuring and institutional integration – a legacy of organisational adaptation and cultural change that has remained invisible in much of the public debate. The most significant changes have been:[41]

O   the integration of many smaller exam boards, both academic and vocational, into just three 'unitary awarding bodies' for England: Edexcel (created in 1996), OCR (1998) and AQA (1998)

O   the creation of a single regulator (the QCA) for both academic and vocational assessment, curriculum and qualifications in 1997.

This restructuring was driven by both political and commercial logics. Politically, the desire to bridge the gap between formal education and work-based skills provision (reflected in the reorganisation of Whitehall to create the Department for Education and Employment in the mid-1990s) provided a similar rationale for integrating the provision and regulation of academic and vocational qualifications. Commercially, it reflected the growing importance of education as a strategic economic sector, in terms of both domestic consumption and export. The prospect of gaining competitive advantage in the growing global market for new educational products and qualifications meant that the acquisition and exploitation of market share became a priority for the whole assessment industry. Merging the exam boards into just three awarding bodies was the obvious way to achieve that. Achieving a comparative advantage in the development of educational products was acknowledged as an important issue for QCA in its Quinquennial Review.[42]

These twin logics reflect the fact that the exam boards are themselves unusual organisational hybrids – they have charitable status but are also listed companies. As the volume of testing has continued to expand, the commercial aspects of the exam boards' operations have attracted growing attention. Yet the costs of designing, organising and marking new exams mean that the exam boards in fact *lose* money on every A-level, and only make good some of their losses through the provision of vocational qualifications.

The ambiguous status of the exam boards is most problematic when it comes to the design and operation of effective regulatory frameworks for qualifications, where a number of regulatory dilemmas (some more familiar than others) present themselves:

O   Like the privatised public utilities, the qualifications framework implies a kind of 'universal service obligation' on the exam boards to provide awards even when it is not economically viable to do so. For the exam boards, however, this loss-making function is the core part of their business.

O   The rationale for retaining three exam boards rather than merging them into one is quite properly that three boards encourages innovation in design, diversity and security of provision, and greater breadth of choice. Yet, given that any innovation will probably mean losing money, the regulatory framework itself may not be enough to encourage innovation unless it provides other forms of incentives, especially in a situation where government and regulator are under pressure to demonstrate continuity with the past and to inject more checks and controls into the system.

O   The absence of major price competition creates a perverse incentive to make products more attractive by lowering standards.[43] It can also mean that costs for schools remain artificially high. The Tomlinson Report revealed that the cost of exams varied considerably between the three boards, yet schools did not feel that price corresponded to the quality of the service they received. At the same time, harmonising costs would, under current arrangements, run the risk of infringing anti-cartel laws.[44]

Whether and if so how much these pressures are adversely affecting the performance of the system is unclear. There is no evidence to suggest that QCA's quality assurance procedures are defective enough to allow them to impact on the standards of exams themselves.[45] But that has not prevented mounting concern being expressed, particularly by politicians, about the capacity of existing regulatory structures and institutions to cope with the dilemmas which this ambiguity poses.[46] This difficulty has been exacerbated by the perceived problem of government having a vested interest in improving standards, as measured by exam results; those suspicious of or disgruntled with the system are able to claim that government cannot be entirely objective when its main goal is to demonstrate progress towards its self-imposed performance targets.

> ### Box 4 Key concepts: cohort-referencing, norm-referencing and criterion-referencing
>
> How students' performance should be graded to best maintain standards has been a focus of much of the discussion of the recent A-level debacle. At the heart of the problem is the question of what students' performance is compared or *referenced* against, which is much more difficult to answer than might be expected.
>
> One often cited solution is to allocate a certain proportion of students taking a test to each grade – eg the top 10% get an A, the next 10% get a B, and so on. This is known as 'cohort-referencing'. This approach is sometimes confused with 'norm-referencing'. In fact, there is an important distinction between the two. Norm-referencing compares the results of an individual with those of a

clearly defined group that has been assessed *in the past*. In some cases this will be a one-off control group, in others the previous year's cohort.

Both approaches provide a very visible, but highly questionable, form of continuity over time. All they do is to limit the numbers of each grade that are awarded, without doing anything to preserve the standard required to achieve that grade. This would in fact fluctuate from year to year depending on the overall ability of that cohort. It would also vary depending on the distribution of marks within a particular subject, creating an unfair situation in which there are very few marks separating an A grade from a E grade in one subject and a much wider gap in another. In terms of the management of the education system as a whole, it enables no conclusions to be drawn about improvements in student (and therefore school) performance over time. Perhaps most importantly, it is based on a crude and fundamentally elitist conception of performance. As Wiliam argues, 'it is very easy to place candidates in rank order, without having any clear idea of what they are being put in rank order of'.[47]

The alternative is 'criterion-referenced' assessment, in which students are assessed against clearly defined learning objectives. The advantage of this is that it forces us to be much more explicit and specific about what we are trying to assess and the learning outcomes we want students to achieve. It is also fairer, in that all those deemed to have met a predetermined standard are recognised for having done so. But criterion-referencing is not as straightforward as it may seem. First, all criteria are based on an underlying normative judgement, otherwise they would not make sense. Second, no matter how tightly specified the criteria, marking depends on the subjective professional judgement of markers. Some kind of norm-referencing is an important tool for helping markers to ensure they are marking consistently from year to year.[48]

Free-riding

The task of those responsible for delivering assessment both in schools and in the exam boards has been made immeasurably more difficult by the growing incidence of 'free-riding' on the school system. The principal culprit has been the higher education sector. The distortionary impact that the higher education timetable imposes on school exams is well known, and the Tomlinson Report raised the prospect of moving towards a post-qualifications admission system as a means of reducing pressure on the system.[49] The tone of the recent higher education white paper suggested that government is sympathetic to this idea.[50]

But this practical issue should not distract attention from the underlying problem that universities in the UK have allowed themselves to become overly dependent on the standardised performance information that schools and public examinations provide. Beyond the elite universities, systematic interviewing of prospective candidates is now the exception not the rule. There is no British equivalent of the SAT used by American universities, or the specialised core skills tests taken by all candidates for university entrance in Queensland, Australia.[51] Scholarship programmes are nowhere near as widespread in the UK as they are in the US, closing off another channel for attracting particular kinds of talent. In short, higher education massively underinvests in systems of knowledge certification customised to its needs, and instead free-rides on the school system to identify and select potential students. Of course, the A-level was originally designed to allow schools to perform exactly that function – to filter out the relatively small group of each age cohort that would go on to higher education. But that was half a century ago. Given how the position of the A-level has changed, with new patterns of schooling and educational participation and the growing importance of higher-level qualifications in the labour market, it is time to re-evaluate the kinds of information assessment can and should be expected to provide.

It is important not to underestimate the extent to which this focus on sorting students for university entrance distorts the effective operation of the assessment system and the education system more widely. In the first place, what universities choose to privilege as assessment information then further conditions the behaviour of the rest of the system. It means that schools are measured primarily in terms of their ability to get students good grades, thus entrenching an unhelpful focus on test results themselves rather than the wider processes of learning and development that underpin them. Second, by reducing the A-level qualification to a points score it further undermines the notion that passing it 'qualifies' you to do anything. Like the GCSEs, A-levels have become simply a passport to further learning. The question is whether they are really the best design for this passport.

The debate about access and admissions that has arisen around university funding in recent years, particularly in light of proposals to charge extra tuition fees, in a way reflects a growing recognition that a crude system of allocating points to particular grades is unsustainable. This is particularly important when pressure on the sector to expand and widen participation makes the task of distinguishing between students on the basis of their exam grades more and more difficult for universities. Paradoxically, however, there is a danger that in order to cope with the volume of applications and to be seen to be fair in dealing with them, universities become *more* not less reliant on the kind of comparative, universally available but ultimately impoverished data that A-level grades provide. At the moment the signs are rather mixed. On the one hand, the *Fair Enough?* project launched by Universities UK has begun to think about how objective criteria related to likely academic success – such as self-management – could be used to make the admissions process more valid and inclusive. On the other hand, there has also been considerable interest in the scope for using decontextualised cognitive ability tests like the American SAT, or even the standardised uniform marks provided to A-level students, to enable finer differentiation between students. The question is whether an alternative assessment system could achieve both greater validity, fitness-for-purpose *and* transparency and inter-operability.

Rising expectations

The final piece of the jigsaw, and the key to understanding why institutional adaptation has still struggled to accommodate such a major expansion in provision, is radical change in the nature of public and political expectations of the assessment and qualifications system. Perhaps the most accurate way of capturing how this dynamic has played out would be to frame it not in terms of rising expectations *per se*, but rather a growing intolerance of failure. Indeed, it is probably true to say that this intolerance of failure marks out the education system, or at least the visible and exposed part of the education system of which assessment and qualifications is an integral part, from other large scale public services.

One obvious explanation for this is that assessment has become more and more 'high-stakes': the information that assessment provides is used to make decisions whose impact on the lives and careers of learners, teachers – and ministers – is felt to be increasingly profound. However, it is also clear that the structure of the assessment regime militates against the flawless performance that such high stakes demand. Even if the exam boards were to achieve a reliability rate of 99.9 per cent, that would still equate to tens of thousands of mistakes a year. Estelle Morris, former Secretary of State for Education and Skills, suggested that this level of performance was unsatisfactory, since 'one mistake is always going to be one too many for the individual concerned'.[52] Of course, errors will inevitably be very regrettable as far as those individuals affected are concerned. But no system on the scale or complexity of the assessment system as it is currently constituted could conceivably reduce failure much beyond this level – to expect it to smacks of what management theorists sometimes call 'we need a bigger hammer' syndrome.[53]

Nevertheless, the high stakes involved are an insufficient explanation for why intolerance of failure is so great. After all, the decisions taken in some of the other public services really are life-and-death, yet public tolerance of failure seems to be much greater. (For example, in a landmark study, Chassin showed how the public are prepared to tolerate astonishing levels of risk and error in healthcare provision that would be simply inconceivable in other activities and enterprises).[54] A more plausible explanation could be that assessment is basically seen as a much less complex process than a medical procedure, and therefore mistakes are seen as less excusable. Ironically, this may well have been aggravated by the new rules on returning scripts introduced from 1999. Intended to make the process of marking more transparent, this had the effect of demystifying the process to many, while simultaneously increasing the opportunity to challenge the grade awarded.

But if it is the emergent properties of the assessment system that make it so logistically complex, and not the process of delivering an assessment itself, this raises an important and subversive question. Why, if the process of delivering an assessment is itself relatively simple (ie a teacher can design, organise and mark a classroom test very easily), have we allowed the way the vast majority of assessment is delivered to become so complex? This question is explored further in the next chapter.

A dual imperative

Qualifications and their administration are thus faced with dual, competing imperatives. On the one hand, they must do more of the same: helping to meet demand for increased standards and for maintaining the quality and credibility of a system that is subject to many changes in the wider environment. On the other hand, they must adapt to growing demands to accommodate difference and create more flexible, individualised arrangements for being assessed and awarded with qualifications. The danger is that in the struggle to protect the superficial credibility of the qualifications framework, we have neglected critical thinking about the deeper assessment processes that underpin them. The result, as the next chapter suggests, is that the basic methods of the assessment system have lost their fitness-for-purpose.

5. Basic methods and fitness-for-purpose

The story that has emerged so far is of an assessment and qualifications system, already struggling to cope with multiple perspectives on performance, being forced to accommodate a series of fundamental changes to both the internal structure of the system and the external environment in which it operates. Yet the surprising twist in this story is that despite these changes, the basic methods by which assessment for qualification is delivered, and the process of examining through which it is organised, have changed very little in 50 years. Most is still done:

O   through decontextualised, paper and pencil formats
O   on an individual rather than team basis
O   based largely on constructed-response examination questions
O   with external marking and control
O   to deliver standardised evaluations of pupils
O   according to pre-established criteria.

In other words, the adaptive response of the assessment and qualifications system has been to accommodate rising logistical and organisational complexity while preserving a very clear idea – what Senge calls a 'mental model'[55] – of what assessment should look like. This mental model clearly owes a great deal to the intellectual dominance of the 'scientific measurement' movement in the early twentieth century. The idea that techniques like psychometric testing could be used to select and place people in appropriate roles to promote 'social efficiency' has left a powerful imprint on modern assessment practices. As Shepard argues:

> Dominant theories of the past continue to operate as the default framework affecting current practices and perspectives. Belief systems of teachers, parents, and policy makers are not exact reproductions of formal theories…Nonetheless, formal theories often influence implicit theories held and acted on by these various groups; and because it is difficult to articulate or confront formal theories once they have become a part of the popular culture, their influence may be potent but invisible long after they are abandoned by theorists.[56]

The argument we want to make in this chapter is that preserving this received understanding has just about worked as a survival strategy, in that it has enabled the system to adapt its organisational arrangements to accommodate the logistical complexity imposed on it, but that this success has been bought at a heavy price. It has precluded any real discussion of the role of assessment in validating and privileging certain kinds of knowledge over others, and by increasing the use of externalised methods and reporting it has eroded trust in the professional judgement of education practitioners to deliver assessment in other contexts. Above all, it has had increasingly serious consequences for the system's overall fitness-for-purpose. We focus on three key issues:

○ the validity and reliability of current assessments
○ the evaluative function they are expected to perform
○ the impact of existing methods and systems on the motivation and well-being of learners.

Validity and reliability in educational assessment

Although the social engineering undertones of our modes of assessment have receded somewhat, the influence of the scientific measurement school lingers on in our cultural attachment to the ritual of timed papers sat in an exam hall under strict supervision, which is indicative of a desire to replicate the controlled conditions of the laboratory. The appearance of fairness has always been crucial to the credibility of assessment in 'high-stakes' contexts,[57] and relying on the expert judgement of external examiners has been seen as the best way to defend this claim to fairness. And this has become even more crucial today, when growing pressure for higher standards and greater accountability over the last two decades has increased the range and penetration of high stakes tests within the education system.

But this determination to create what Delandshere calls 'an allure of objectivity'[58] may also help to explain a traditional tendency to emphasise and prioritise the *reliability* of assessment over its *validity* (see Box 5). There is, most people would accept, an inevitable trade-off between the two, although that is not to say that its impact cannot be mitigated through different assessment methods. So it is something of a moral judgement (albeit perhaps an implicit one) about whether, to put it crudely, it is fairer to be equally unfair to everybody, by designing assessments that prioritise reliability over validity, than to risk being fair to some and unfair to others, by designing assessments that prioritise validity over reliability.

> ### Box 5 Key concepts: validity and reliability
>
> 'Validity' relates to the extent to which assessments measure what they are supposed to measure: how deeply connected are they to the forms of knowledge and understanding for which they act as proxies? Although earlier scholars sought to differentiate between different types of validity, most now suggest that validity is best understood as a unitary construct in which it is the *inferences* that are allowed to be drawn from an assessment, rather than the design of the assessment itself, which make it valid or invalid. This is particularly important when it comes to assessment for certification.
>
> Reliability is essentially concerned with whether a test is measuring the same thing on different occasions and with different people or, to put it another way, whether the score someone gets on a test on a particular occasion reflects their 'true' capability.[59] So, for example, the specific questions that are chosen

for a paper could mean that a student performs better or worse than if a different set of questions had been chosen to assess that domain, or a student may perform better or worse from one day to the next. Because reliability is difficult to prove in practical terms, it is usually expressed as an abstract statistical concept that reflects the probability that a student's score on a particular test reflects their 'true' score. Most educational assessments have a reliability of 85 per cent, meaning that on the majority of occasions a candidate with a true score of 50 will get a score of somewhere between 45 and 55.[60]

Validity and reliability are often seen to be in tension. For example, setting tests under controlled conditions may ensure the test is more reliable, but because these conditions have a differential impact on those taking it, these will make it less valid. While most people would accept that assessment must tap deep understanding, rather than superficial knowledge of facts or the ability to repeat isolated skills, this can be undermined by demands for objectivity, particularly in high-stakes contexts. In *How People Learn*, Bransford et al accept that 'much work needs to be done to minimise the trade-off between assessing depth and assessing objectively'.[61]

The argument for poor validity

Let us start by considering the case against the current arrangements on the grounds of their poor validity, which is both easier, since this is explicitly not what they seek to defend, and more important, since it goes to the heart of the kinds of knowledge and understanding we want learners to develop through the curriculum.

The first problem is that traditional methods privilege certain kinds of knowledge over others, because the learning that students are able to demonstrate is limited to that which can be recreated individually using a pen and paper under timed, controlled conditions. One obvious example is that current arrangements reinforce a tendency for learners to be assessed as individuals, and on individual performance, even on forms of ability that are primarily used in team or social settings. Teamwork and other interpersonal skills are highly valued, not least by employers, but they are difficult to demonstrate under typical exam conditions. They are, of course, comparatively easy for teachers' to assess on the basis of their classroom observation.

An emphasis on reliability has meant that many of the means for making assessment tasks more like real life have been closed off to enable standardisation, aggregation and the appearance of scientific objectivity. Decontextualisation means that few assessments test learners' ability to apply their knowledge in appropriate situations. Most tasks have become, in Glaser and Baxter's terms, 'content-lean, process-constrained' in that they do not require significant prior conceptual knowledge and mainly assess learners' ability to follow instructions rather than to explore and represent problems and devise strategies for solving them.[62] This also tends to rule out what this report has identified as a central feature of most problems, namely the possibility of multiple interpretations. In short, 'we start out with the intention of making the important measurable, and end up making the measurable important', as Wiliam has succinctly put it.[63]

Perhaps most seriously, many exams test surface knowledge but not deep understanding or higher-order thinking skills. The only way these can be assessed is through the inclusion of much more complex tasks, taking at least one to two hours to complete – what Resnick and Resnick call 'authentic assessments'[64] – which directly measure the kinds of performance in which we are interested. One example is using practicals in science subjects, rather than relying on written assessments, which stand as rather poor proxies for them. The problem is that at least six such authentic assessments would need to be made to ensure that they were reliable,[65] and this would be much too time-consuming to be fitted into conventional externalised methods. This again suggests that to improve its validity for high-stakes, summative purposes, more assessment needs to take place in the classroom.

A more controversial extension of this argument has been made by Dylan Wiliam in relation to the question of 'teaching to the test'. He has argued that we cannot be sure whether improvements in test scores really reflect improvements in students' performance across the curriculum, or simply in those aspects which are tested. Given the evidence that teachers can predict which aspects of the curriculum are likely to come up in the tests, his contention is that teachers have simply got better at teaching to the test: 'while the *reported* standards of achievement may rise, the actual level of achievement across the whole subject could well be falling'.[66] Although there is no conclusive proof that this is the case, there is considerable circumstantial evidence. The most compelling is from the USA, where states that have changed their standardised tests have found that results initially plummet, then gradually rise to previous levels before plateauing once again.[67] There is also survey evidence from the teaching unions, with one survey suggesting that two-thirds of teachers feel pressured to teach to the test to the detriment of their practice.[68] Finally there is evidence of the distortionary impact of similar target-based performance regimes in other public services, such as the NHS.[69] All this suggests that, at the very least, we should entertain the possibility that alternative approaches to assessment might be superior.

The argument for poor reliability

Although we have suggested that poor validity ought properly to be seen as the more serious problem, there is little doubt that in political terms the sustainability of the current arrangements depends most on their claim to reliability. Any suggestion of poor reliability could undermine public trust in the current arrangements, and we are therefore reluctant to draw any sweeping conclusions in the absence of rigorous empirical evidence. However, there are a number of grounds for concern that must be highlighted.

First, poor marking clearly poses one potential threat to reliability. Indeed, this has been the focus of the recent concerns about reliability, particularly in relation to the marking of the summer 2002 A-levels. Specifically, it was alleged that students sitting an exam set by one particular exam board had been marked differently from those sitting a different paper from a different exam board in the same subject. More generally, it is not uncommon for exam boards to identify 'rogue-markers', examiners whose marking is erratic and therefore impossible to moderate on a statistical basis. However, the boards have established procedures for identifying and dealing with rogue-markers, and marking is in fact a much less important factor in reliability than the recent furore suggested.[70] Its impact could be further minimised through the implementation of some of the recommendations and ideas in the Tomlinson Report, notably providing more time for marking, better systems for catching rogue-markers earlier and more cross-referencing through greater use of examiners from other awarding bodies.[71]

Nevertheless, there are potentially much more serious reliability issues inherent to the design of external exams themselves. Two are particularly salient: first, the extent to which external exams rely on a snapshot of a learner's performance on a given day; and, second, the classification of marks into grades or levels. Let us consider each in turn.

The first problem is that rather than basing our assessments on the learning and skills students demonstrate over hundreds of hours in the classroom, we rely on the snapshot provided by their performance in (at most) a few hours of exams at the end of a course. This means that exams are subject to two main sources of error. A student may perform better or worse depending on the actual questions chosen for the paper that year, or the student may perform better or worse from one day to the next. In terms of the former, the error relates to how well the test samples from the curriculum (with regard to both content and the type of performance required). It can therefore be made more reliable by making tests longer. But this is easier said than done. To increase the reliability of a test from 90 per cent reliable to 95 per cent reliable the number of items would need to be doubled. To increase the reliability from 85 per cent to 95 per cent, the number of items would have to more than tripled.[72] In terms of the latter, it is very difficult to say how significant a source of error this is, but few who have taken exams could not recount at least one occasion when for whatever reason they did not 'do themselves justice'. Intuitively, therefore, it seems likely to be fairly significant.

In both cases, of course, the instinctive response of many people might be 'tough luck'. We seem to have a powerful cultural attachment to the idea that the top performers naturally rise to the occasion, and that ability to perform under the stress of an external exam is a robust proxy for ability to perform well in stressful workplace situations. But not only is the empirical basis of this claim never produced to support it, it also runs counter to the logic that we would apply in many other situations. For example, when deciding whether to award an employee a promotion, would a rational employer base his or her decision on their observation of the candidate over two hours one Thursday afternoon, or on their performance over the course of the last year?

The second problem requires that we look more closely at how reliability is measured. As in the illustration above, reliability is usually expressed as a statistical construct ('85 per cent reliability', etc). But a number of scholars have suggested that to state the figures in this way is somewhat misleading because it conflates the reliability of the *mark* given for a particular test with the accuracy of the *grade* awarded for performance on that test.[73] This does not reflect the way that results are actually used – marks are sorted and aggregated into a smaller number of grades, amplifying the problem for those students where a wrong mark drags them across a grade boundary.

Put bluntly, what this means is that on most tests a large number of candidates are awarded the wrong grade. This would not necessarily matter if we were more honest about the uncertainty of grading but, as the pressure on universities to accept growing numbers of students and to differentiate between students on the basis of increasingly tiny margins has increased, we have come to put *more* not less faith in single grades, which can now mean the difference between a student going to their first-choice university or not. Exact figures are difficult to ascertain because figures for reliability are not routinely provided, but it has been estimated that between one-fifth and two-fifths of candidates in NCTs, GCSEs and A-levels could be being awarded the wrong grade or level (some lower, some higher, and a few two grades higher or lower).[74]

Evaluative function

The corollary of these problems with validity and reliability is that the evaluative function that assessment performs becomes problematic. This discussion is primarily focused on that component of the assessment system, the National Curriculum Tests, which has an explicitly evaluative function. But informal decisions about schools may also be based on their students' GCSE and A-level results, so concerns about these results may be equally applicable.

In theory, NCTs enable the performance of schools to be measured and compared, and improvements in the education system to be tracked over time. The great strength of the current system is its transparency and simple coherence. The scores awarded to students in NCTs are routinely aggregated to get the scores for a whole school, which can then be compared through league tables to guide parental choice. Ultimately these can be further aggregated to arrive at a national level of attainment for that cohort, which allows ministers and voters to keep track of improvements in the education system as a whole.

But this coherence is ultimately also its major weakness. The same set of data is expected to serve both a summative function for individual pupils and an evaluative function for schools (note that very little formative value can be extracted because it is impossible to disaggregate summative data). The problem is that the high-stakes evaluative function squeezes out the relatively low-stakes summative function. To put it another way, a student's score on Key Stage tests does not matter much to the student. If it didn't matter to teachers or schools either, then we could safely assume that test results were a good indication of progress across the full range of the curriculum, because neither teachers nor learners would have any real incentive to narrow their focus to what was likely to appear in the test. However, since this is not the case, teachers have an incentive to focus their teaching on what is likely to be tested, and the tests cease to be a useful measure of the quality of the teaching and learning going on in a school. As Wiliam argues,[75] this seems to confirm Goodhart's Law that performance indicators lose their usefulness when used as objects of policy.

It is important to emphasise that teaching to the test *per se* is not the problem. Indeed, evaluative assessment should be designed so that we are happy for teachers to teach to the test because the tests themselves were a broad representation of the desired curriculum. Our current system does not satisfy these conditions, and this leads to the pertinent question of whether a single assessment system can ever serve multiple purposes. Few scholars believe that this is the case, not least because the design of the assessment usually betrays the priorities of those that have designed it. For evaluative purposes, for example, it is useful for a student's results to be aggregated to a single number or grade, whereas for summative purposes it should properly capture a more complex range of performances.

Impact on learners' motivation and well-being

The final part of our critique, but in many ways the most important, in light of our vision of assessment being about 'making learners better learners', relates to the impact that current assessment arrangements are having on the motivation to learn and the well-being of learners.

The view that testing raises standards of educational achievement rests on the assumption that increasing the transparency of performance motivates teachers and students to put more effort into their teaching and learning. When we are shown that our performance is inadequate, our response (so the argument runs) is to declare, like Boxer the industrious horse in *Animal Farm*, 'I will work harder'.[76] Yet, however intuitively appealing this logic may seem, it rests on a largely fictional – or at best very elitist – account of what motivates us to learn.

This has been confirmed in a systematic review of the evidence of the impact of testing on students' motivation. It found that, despite the rhetorical commitment to 'lifelong learning', current approaches to assessment are only developing motivation towards performance goals, not learning goals. Passing exams has come to be seen as an end in itself, rather than as part of a process of preparing for real-life challenges. This is inhibiting *all* students, even high-performers, in developing the skills and the orientation for continuous learning.[77] As Black and Wiliam put it, 'where the classroom culture focuses on rewards, "gold stars", grades or place-in-the-class ranking, then pupils look for the ways to obtain the best marks rather than at the needs of their learning which these marks ought to reflect'.[78] This does not bode well for a future in which learners will have to be much more self-aware and much more adept at planning and managing their own learning throughout their lives.

Moreover, tests only work in motivating some students, primarily those who were already high-achievers, thereby increasing inequality between students. Low-achievers, however, tend to be overwhelmed by the volume of assessment and demotivated by being constantly reminded of their low achievement. Harlen and Deakin-Crick conclude that 'a greater emphasis on summative assessment thus brings about increased differentiation'.[79] This conclusion seems to be supported by the UK's performance in the PISA study (see Appendix 4). Although the overall picture was quite positive, in that the UK was one of only nine countries to score significantly above the OECD average in all three domains that were assessed (reading, mathematical and scientific literacy), the difference in performance between high and low achievers in the UK was one of the most marked in the study.

This may be because the effort students invest in tasks is related to the feedback they received from earlier performance on similar tasks. If lower-achieving students are made to feel like failures, it not only reduces their motivation for current learning activities but, by damaging their self-esteem, reduces future effort (and therefore chances of success).

There is also evidence that tests distort teachers' classroom practices to the detriment of learners. In high-stakes contexts, teachers are not only tempted to 'teach to the test' but tend to adopt a 'transmission' style of teaching. This puts learners with different preferred learning styles at a disadvantage and damages their self-esteem. The use of repeated practice tests reinforces the low self-image of the lower-achieving students.

Potentially most seriously, there is evidence that tests damage children's physical and mental well-being. Before the introduction of NCTs there was no correlation between the achievement of students and their self-esteem. Afterwards, low-achieving pupils had lower self-esteem than higher-achieving pupils. Students dislike high-stakes tests, preferring other forms of assessment. Students, particularly girls, also show high levels of test anxiety.[80] A recent Department of Health study showed the consequences that this anxiety can have: 11–15-year-olds who did not think they were going to live up to the expectations of others in terms of their exam performance were most likely to have the highest drug use.[81]

The review found no evidence to suggest that these effects improved as children got older and more familiar with testing; on the contrary, older students feel more 'resentment, anxiety, cynicism and mistrust' towards standardised tests, perhaps as they become more aware of how much is riding on them. Nor does it seem to make much difference to the impact on learners whether the tests are primarily about assessing individuals (eg the 11-plus) or about assessing schools (eg NCTs).

Summing up

To summarise the argument so far, we have painted a picture of an assessment and qualifications system struggling to accommodate increasingly intense pressure on its underlying processes and arrangements. The task of adapting to these new demands has been made more difficult by the existence of multiple and often competing perspectives on the system's performance, with no easy way of prioritising or negotiating between them. The way that the system has sought to cope has been to preserve a particular received wisdom about the specific characteristics of robust assessment methods. In doing so, the system has managed to deliver traditional forms of assessment on an ever larger and more complex scale, but only by seriously impairing its fitness-for-purpose.

Another way of thinking about these ideas is suggested by Senge et al,[82] who use the metaphor of the 'Iceberg' to help chart an analytical path from the practical and immediate (particular events that have happened recently) through several levels of abstraction (including patterns and systemic structures) to arrive at the underlying values and assumptions on which the system depends.

In the case of assessment and qualifications, following this analytical path is very important because it helps to illustrate the ways in which organisational arrangements, functions and basic methods are stitched together by a certain mental model of assessment. It follows that re-imagining the system must begin by building an alternative mental model that can form the kernel for a new assessment paradigm. This is the task of the next chapter.

6. Towards a scientific revolution in assessment

The central implication of the analysis so far is that assessment urgently requires a 'scientific revolution' of the kind envisaged by Kuhn.[83] This chapter argues that an emergent and increasingly coherent set of ideas and evidence about how people learn should be the basis for a long-term, root and branch restructuring of qualifications and the models of assessment that underpin them. We briefly sketch the contribution that assessment can make to learning, and then set out how this contribution might be reflected in a set of organisational arrangements that together constitute an alternative assessment and qualifications paradigm.

The importance of this to the wider thrust of education reform is profound. As the earlier discussion of alignment made clear, changes in the curriculum and pedagogy will only be meaningful and sustainable if they are accompanied by complementary changes in assessment practices, and vice versa. A new approach to assessment must therefore ask: what is it that we want from the curriculum over the next period of reform, and is such a conception underpinned by robust theories of learning and pedagogy?

Theory of learning

Arguably the most significant trend in educational research in recent decades has been an emerging consensus around 'constructivist' theories of learning. Constructivism (as its name suggests) contends that all new knowledge is 'constructed' on the basis of current knowledge and that learners understand better when they are actively involved in constructing the knowledge that they are learning, and in integrating it into their existing knowledge base. Contrary to some misperceptions, however, this does not mean that advocates of constructivism think that only the process of learning is important, that content is irrelevant or superficial, or that disciplinary boundaries and structures should be ignored.

The most comprehensive assessment of evidence, undertaken in the USA by the Committee on Developments in the Science of Learning, confirms that constructivist insights remain the basic foundation of what we know about how people learn.[84] A detailed examination of constructivist learning theory is beyond the scope of this report,[85] but a brief overview reveals five core concepts.

First, how we construct new knowledge and understanding depends on what we *already* know and believe. Even very young learners bring existing points of view to any new learning setting, which they use to help interpret and process the new information they receive. Learners actively teach themselves what this information means, how it fits with what they already know, whether it makes sense in terms of their existing understanding, and how they might need to rethink other related ideas to accommodate this new knowledge.[86] Uncovering these mental models is very important because otherwise understanding may not develop in the way anticipated by the teacher.[87]

Second, this process of bringing existing understandings to the surface and helping the learner to see how they might need to be changed is one illustration of the profoundly *social* basis of learning. Learning develops through social interactions that provide learners with opportunities to develop new skills and understanding with guidance, support and 'scaffolding' from an adult or more proficient peer.

Third, the value of transferring knowledge learned in one context and using it new contexts is one of the basic building blocks of our education system, whether this transfer is from one task to another, from one year to another, from the classroom to the workplace or community. Indeed, it is why we aim to 'educate' people rather than simply to 'train' them for specific tasks.[88] How knowledge is *organised* is absolutely critical to our ability to use it in other contexts. Effective transfer requires deep understanding. Superficial understanding tends to be based on classroom routines or simple memorisation, so that outside these familiar situations learners do not recognise where or how a concept may be relevant. As understanding develops knowledge comes to be organised around increasingly sophisticated, integrated and generalisable principles. One illustration of this has been uncovered by research into what distinguishes experts from novices. Experts do not necessarily know *more* than novices, but they are able to organise different domains of knowledge around 'a specification of the contexts in which it is useful'.[89] This is termed 'conditionalised knowledge', and enables them to access and apply knowledge relevant to different situations much more effectively.

Fourth, constructivist theory has highlighted the importance of *metacognition* in intelligent thinking. Broadly speaking, metacognition means thinking about thinking. It refers to 'people's abilities to predict their performance on various tasks…and to monitor their current levels of mastery and understanding'.[90] Sometimes called the 'learning to learn' skills, metacognitive skills allow learners to take charge of managing their own learning, identifying situations in which to test their understanding, evaluate the results and undertake new learning activity as a result so that new levels of performance are attained without prompting from a teacher.

Finally, it is important to emphasise that none of this evidence implies a content-free curriculum. On the contrary, it is clear that subject matter knowledge is an essential prerequisite for profound and effective learning. To stress the importance of problem-solving skills (say) is not to pretend that the skills for solving a complex algebra problem are the same as those required for constructing a causal claim about a particular historical event since, self-evidently, mathematics and history involve different approaches to enquiry and argumentation and rest on different content. As Bransford et al note, 'expertise in particular areas involves more than a set of general problem-solving skills; it also requires well-organised knowledge of *concepts* and *inquiry procedures* pertinent to that subject' (emphasis added).[91] And as Howard Gardner suggests, our educational subjects and disciplines (whatever their imperfections and inadequacies) have emerged in their present form precisely because they represent our best efforts to think systematically about the world.[92]

What this highlights is the importance of 'teaching for understanding', where curriculum and pedagogy are focused on depth rather than breadth. Developing learners' modes of thinking – the key concepts, enquiry procedures and problem-solving skills they need in different subjects – by focusing on a few topics in detail is much more important than covering a large volume of content but never having the opportunity to interrogate it in depth or to develop skills that will be more widely applicable. Another way of putting this is that we should not try to teach students history (for example), but rather to teach them to think like historians.

The opportunities and challenges for assessment

This set of concepts has potentially very wide-reaching implications for assessment and its place within the wider context of educational practice. We focus here on two, the first a challenge, the second an opportunity. The first is **that assessment systems need to be fundamentally re-designed to test deep understanding rather than just content knowledge**. Many assessments currently fail to determine properly whether knowledge is conditionalised or whether it remains 'inert', ie whether learners understand when and how to activate it. Glaser and Baxter provide a useful schema with which to judge assessment tasks against their stated objectives.[93] Assessments can be understood, they argue, in terms of their content demands (to what extent does the task require prior knowledge or is most necessary information provided?) and their process demands (to what extent are students expected to generate their own processes for solving problems or are they given explicit instructions?) of the tasks involved.

Assessing for understanding would mean rejecting a number of key features of the prevailing mental model of assessment outlined in the previous chapter. Foremost among them is the notion that assessment can be designed and carried out without the active participation of classroom teachers. To be a valid test of deep understanding, assessment tasks must be authentic, requiring both knowledge of key concepts and processes within that subject area. To be reliable, there must be at least six of them, drawn from the topics teachers have chosen to focus on in depth. *To be both valid and reliable, they must be carried out in the classroom.*

The second is that **we have a great opportunity to recast** assessment not simply as a way of certifying learning, but of actively contributing to it. Assessment has become so synonymous with external testing at the end of a programme of study that we have lost sight of the crucial role that appropriately designed (and delivered) forms of assessment can play in improving the quality of classroom teaching and learning. To put it another way, we need to reassert assessment *for* learning, not just assessment *of* learning. Assessment for learning is what was earlier described as formative. It has been defined as 'the process of seeking and interpreting evidence for use by learners and their teachers to decide where the learners are in their learning, where they need to go and how best to get there' (see Box 6).[94]

> ### Box 6 Assessment for learning
> The Assessment Reform Group has defined ten principles of assessment for learning. According to this framework, assessment for learning:
>
> O   is part of effective planning of teaching and learning
> O   focuses on how students learn, enabling students to become as aware of the 'how' of their learning as they are of the 'what'
> O   is central to classroom practice, because much of what teachers and learners do in the classroom is assessment of one kind or another
> O   is a key professional skill for teachers, that should be supported through initial and continuing professional development
> O   is sensitive and constructive, because it recognises the emotional impact that different kinds of assessment and feedback have on learners
> O   fosters motivation to learn, by emphasising progress and achievement rather than failure
> O   promotes understanding of learning goals and the criteria by which they are assessed
> O   provides learners with constructive guidance about how to improve

> ○ develops learners' capacity for self-assessment so that they
>   can become more self-managing in seeking out new skills,
>   knowledge and understanding
> ○ recognises the full range of achievements of all learners.
>
> Assessment Reform Group[95]

The importance of assessment for learning can be understood in terms of three 'Ms': mental models, motivation and metacognition. First, the research on learning shows frequent formative assessment can play a crucial role in helping to make students' thinking visible to themselves and their teachers, and drawing out the prior understandings (or misunderstandings) on which new knowledge will be constructed. In doing so, it provides invaluable information to guide further teaching and learning in ways that work with rather than against the grain of learners' existing mental models.[96]

Second, assessment for learning proceeds from a recognition of the profound impact that assessment can have on learners' motivation and self-esteem, evidence for which was marshalled in the previous chapter. Fostering motivation means emphasising progress rather than failure. It means providing detailed feedback, encouragement, and constructive advice about how to improve, rather than simply giving grades. Where feedback is provided it encourages a focus on individual learning goals and the formative value that assessment can offer. Where grades are given the focus shifts almost immediately to performance goals, and the potential formative value for the learner is usually lost.

Third, assessment for learning understands the importance of metacognitive skills. It seeks to improve learners' capacity to understand and shape their personal learning goals, what it is they are trying to achieve. It also helps learners to take more responsibility for self-assessment and reflecting on their own performance, and using these judgements to determine their priorities for further learning. It encourages learners to think about *how* they learn as well as *what* they learn.

Even within the design constraints of the existing system, **assessment** for learning has been found, as a comprehensive review of the evidence by Black and Wiliam concluded unequivocally, to have a dramatic impact on standards of attainment.[97] The size of this impact even on the more pessimistic projections was found to be equivalent to a learner improving their performance by at least one to two grades at GCSE level. Replicated across the national cohort, it would move the UK from a middle ranking in the Third International Mathematics and Science Study (TIMSS) to the top five. Needless to say, this constitutes an impact more profound than could be claimed for most educational interventions.

Moreover, Black and Wiliam found that much could be done to improve the contribution that teachers' assessment practices made to learning, in respect of three main problems: first, that teachers' assessment practices are often ineffective in promoting good learning; second, that marking and grading tends to focus learners on competition and rank rather than scope for personal improvement; and third, that assessment feedback often has a negative impact, particularly on low achievers.[98]

Wider implications

This review has necessarily been brief, but it nonetheless illustrates how realigning assessment strategies and award structures to support the central principles of teaching for understanding, assessing for learning, and developing a system that aims to develop more effective learners could have a radical impact on the achievement and motivation of students. As we have seen, the set of functions that qualifications and assessment data have taken on over the decades does not always correspond with these goals. But assessment for learning is not incompatible with many of the other objectives and needs that the current school system tries to serve. In fact, if developed properly, assessment for learning could become a source of coherence and energy for broader efforts to improve standards, tackle underachievement and bring out the full potential of all students:

O   By improving and certifying ability to learn, it would allow the assessment and qualifications system to be reshaped to serve the key strategic function of school-age education in the twenty-first century.

○ By highlighting the contribution assessment can make to powerful learning, it would embed assessment in the practices of teachers, learners and schools without defining the parameters of their activities.

○ By recognising the value of teacher assessment, it would enable assessment for summative purposes to be both more valid and more reliable.

○ By re-emphasising the robustness of assessments carried out in classrooms and schools, it would reduce the logistical complexity of the assessment system and its dependence on an over-stretched, centralised external marking process.

○ By cutting down on external assessment, it would also free up resources. Suppose that we were to cut the external assessment bill for each school in half: it would free up £50,000 to be spent on more important learning resources – teachers, specialist consultants, ICTs, books and so on.

○ By reclaiming assessment for learners, it would better prepare all those that pass through it for a career as a lifelong learner.

7. A new vision for assessment and qualifications: principles, consequences and strategies

The last chapter laid the theoretical ground for a new approach to assessment. This chapter illustrates how this broad set of ideas might be translated into a radically new vision for assessment and qualifications. Quite deliberately, this is presented more as a provocation than as a detailed blueprint, for two reasons. First, being unduly prescriptive about the details of reform can detract from the coherence of the overall vision. Second, trying to pre-empt the many specific decisions that need to be made for this vision to be realised risks distracting attention from the key strategic political choices that must be made first.

If we can establish the long-term trajectory that the system should follow, and identify the essential features that should define a reshaped system in the future, then more detailed and specific aspects of it can emerge through innovation and experimentation among users, practitioners, researchers and others.

For this to happen, however, a degree of certainty about the direction of travel, and about government's commitment to seeing the journey through to its end, is required. Without it, it is difficult to see how the traditional inertia of the assessment system, and to a lesser extent the qualifications system, will be overcome.

The government has announced its intention to develop a unified award framework in the medium to long term. In many respects, this is the culmination of repeated attempts to bridge the gap between academic and vocational qualifications, and between the classroom and work-based learning that underpins them.

What the proposals do not yet address is the challenge of developing an assessment system that is fit for this purpose, and which does not repeat the historic tendency of seeking to engineer 'parity of esteem' between different routes by making the modes of assessing vocational learning more like those traditionally used for academic learning. The idea that you can hammer square pegs into round holes has never, and will never, provide a credible or sustainable solution.

Creating a coherent and seamless set of choices for learners as they progress towards a unified award will depend instead on developing an assessment system that is much more flexible and does not prioritise the knowledge, skills and understanding gained in one context over that gained in another.

In order to do this, we must:

O make explicit the core principles on which a new system would be built
O identify their key implications, both generally and for specific stakeholders
O create the space and the incentives to develop the detailed practices through which more effective modes of assessment and qualification awards might emerge
O develop a set of institutional arrangements that make it possible to implement such practices on a large scale.

The focus of this chapter is primarily on the first two of these points. We begin by setting out the five principles of a new approach.

1. Qualifications should qualify you for something, and that something should be **further learning**.
2. Assessment should combine **the best of academic and vocational practices** in order to certify not just what you know, or what you can do, but how well you learn.

3. Within a decade, everyone should be entitled to receive **a personalised programme of learning** that reflects their individual profile as a learner and which should be assessed appropriately.
4. The purpose of assessment in schools should be to generate authentic and formative data about learners and their future needs, and **other purposes should not be allowed to predominate**.
5. The provision of learning and its validation and certification **should not be a closed shop**.

1. Qualifications should qualify you for something, and that something should be further learning

Learning matters because no one is born with the ability to function competently as an adult. The ability to learn matters more today than it ever has done, because in modern society the demands and expectations we place on the knowledge and skills of workers and citizens have never been greater. Yet few of our national qualifications actively set out to certify the ability to learn. Ironically, even fewer actually qualify those that achieve them for *anything other than* to go on to do some more learning. As a result, they are not fit for the purpose they are expected to serve. It is time to imagine a new assessment and qualifications system which is.

We should start by making ability to learn the foundation of a new approach to assessment. School-based assessment would be reshaped to place much greater emphasis on the use of formative assessment (assessment for learning) to promote both cognitive skills, through deep understanding of subject knowledge, and metacognitive skills, through systematic programmes of 'learning to learn'. Summative assessment (assessment of learning) would be reframed to reflect a more even balance between *what* has been learnt, in terms of knowledge and skills, and *how* it has been learnt, in terms of the development of 'learning to learn' skills. As Gardner suggests,[99] our aim should be to develop students that do not just learn history, but learn to think like a historian; that do not just learn engineering, but learn to think like an engineer.

The qualifications system would be refocused on this primary purpose, through the creation of a single overarching award designed to qualify learners to go on to further learning within their chosen field. This **Learning Licence** would cover the whole of the 14–19 phase. It would build on a set of assessment practices in pre-14 education that are consistent with the principles of assessment for learning, so that from an early age learners become familiar with a form of assessment which is formative of and integral to learning, not semi-detached from it. This overarching principle would not exclude the use of assessment information for other purposes – indeed a more learning-focused approach to assessment could actually help to make this information both more valid and reliable. But the cumulative weight of an assessment portfolio, the combined result of a young person's career in school-age education, should reflect the ability to learn as its central goal.

2. Assessment should combine the best of academic and vocational practices in order to certify not just what you know, or what you can do, but how well you learn

Despite the undisputed strengths of the vocational system, there is little doubt that attempts to engineer parity of esteem from the centre have failed. The current phase of reform, and plans to introduce a unified award framework, run the risk that existing barriers between subject knowledge, disciplines, domains and 'key skills' will simply be imported and resurrected within a newly restructured qualifications framework. The recent proposals for 'hybrid' GCSEs, which once again emphasise the need to make the vocational more academic, rather than vice versa, suggest that government has not yet found a way round this problem.

Focusing qualifications and the assessment underpinning them on the ability to learn is a much more promising way of overcoming the false dichotomies between 'knowledge' and 'skills' and between academic and vocational routes. By enabling a richer, and more varied set of learning opportunities to be assessed by appropriate methods, vocational forms of examination would have a key role to play in a reshaped system alongside traditional academic approaches. Everyone would be entitled to a mode of assessment that combined the best of vocational and academic routes:

forms of examination that reflect context-based performance and expert judgement on the one hand and the ability to marshal more abstract factual knowledge and organise it through coherent disciplinary and conceptual frameworks on the other. Cutting across both would be a focus on how well the ability to learn has been developed within that domain.

Here, the awarding bodies are well positioned to take a lead in examining how elements of vocational and academic awards might be brought together in practice. This challenge provides a clear focus for research and development work to develop and test new instruments for delivering qualifications.

But to work in practice, several other features of the system need to change. Most obvious is the regulatory environment in assessment, which following the events of summer 2002 is currently heavily focused on avoiding errors, tightening central control and making more frequent interventions. The regulatory grip needs to be loosened, and the exam boards given both resources and permission to innovate before we can expect new forms of assessment to emerge.

3. Within a decade, everyone should be entitled to receive a personalised programme of learning that reflects their individual profile as a learner and which should be assessed appropriately

The concept of learner pathways has entered the political lexicon, but has so far been rather vague and aspirational. It is time it was made concrete. Within a decade, the shape of the assessment system and the education system more widely should be restructured to accommodate personalised programmes of learning. This framework would provide scope for general, subject specialist, occupational, vocational, and perhaps ultimately community-based pathways. The system would be designed to optimise flexibility by enabling learners to move both horizontally, between different pathways, and vertically, to higher levels, while also respecting the rigours of different disciplines and specialisms. Adult learners would be able to enter the system at whatever level was appropriate to their needs and experience.

Pathways would enable learners to gain practical experience, and develop knowledge, skills and metacognitive ability customised around these core routes, have them assessed by appropriate methods, and have them reflected and captured in qualifications. Reflecting a greater role for self-management, learners would play a much more active part in determining which modes of assessment were most appropriate.

As far and as fast as possible, assessment for particular components of an award, based on progression through a pathway, should be carried out when a learner is ready for them, and not according to a standard schedule, as is currently the case. Scotland has already gone some way towards assessment on demand. In England, the 14–19 Strategy also points towards this kind of shift in suggesting that GCSE should become more of a mid-way 'progress check' towards an overarching award at 18 or 19.

This will mean systematically stripping away the huge constraints on the ability to undertake assessment on demand imposed by the standardised framework of age cohort progression, by the logistics of exam entry and marking, by the rigid structure of the national curriculum, which requires a certain range of subjects to be taught separately and at specific times, and by the fixed timing of National Curriculum testing and its relatively crude use to monitor the performance and progress of schools. There are some signs of progress in addressing these issues, notably encouragement for schools, LEAs, colleges and Learning and Skills Councils to experiment with new approaches to funding that would allow individual learning pathways to cross the existing boundaries between institutions.

4. The purpose of assessment in schools should be to generate authentic and formative assessment information to shape future teaching and learning, and other purposes should not be allowed to predominate

It is difficult to envisage any sustainable scenario for the assessment system that does not involve much greater emphasis on teachers' classroom assessments. In practical terms, this would make it possible to reduce some of the strain generated by the externalised marking systems currently used to award qualifications. But at a deeper level, teacher assessment clearly has enormous potential both as a way of improving pedagogy and in generating information about pupils that is both more valid and more reliable.

However, at the moment most teachers experience the assessment and qualifications system as more of an 'iron cage' than a structure that underpins and responds to their professional autonomy and development. This has as much to do with the way that assessment information has been used as a lever for improving system performance as with the nature of the assessment itself. Nevertheless, the way that assessments are administered, and the pressure to teach to them that the accountability framework creates, currently acts as a major constraint on the capacity of teachers to produce the accurate, sophisticated and 'just-in-time' assessment information that they are uniquely well placed to provide. The challenge is therefore to find ways of grounding and intertwining the task of giving teachers a more authoritative, productive and empowering role in assessment in the wider process of professional reform, development and restructuring which is already under way in the UK. This does not mean simply transferring responsibility for assessment back to teachers wholesale, not least because teachers often complain that they cannot afford to invest the time that the successful adoption of assessment for learning requires.

Instead, it means exploring the range of ways in which teachers could begin to strengthen the capacity of the whole system to deliver valid and reliable assessment information on demand. But, rather than being seen as an additional burden on an overstretched profession, this incremental rebalancing of the equilibrium between central control and local autonomy should be seen as a further opportunity to restore trust in teachers' professional judgement. Indeed, teachers could become more like the master craftsmen of the historic apprentice system. And by helping students become responsible for managing their own learning, assessment for learning has been found to save teachers' time in the long run. In this way, classroom assessment should be seen not just as part of the solution to the problems of the assessment system, but to some key issues facing the teaching profession more widely in terms of status, workload and recruitment and retention.

5. The provision of learning and its validation and certification should not be a closed shop

Even if its immediate focus is on schools, the long-term evolution of a reshaped assessment and qualifications system should be towards a role in a fully integrated learning society. Current moves to dissolve the boundaries between educational institutions could, taken to their logical conclusion, lead to a much more ambitious attempt to draw together local networks of providers or potential providers of knowledge and learning – from museums and libraries, to rivers and parks, to sports teams and theatre companies, to firms and community organisations. The aim would be that learners could build their pathways around the widest possible range of organisational, digital and cultural resources and experiences.

As this more distributed learning infrastructure takes shape, we should develop modes of assessment that allow this more diverse set of learning experiences to be accredited, rather than allowing the limitations of current assessment methods to determine the learning that takes place. Just as schools will lose their monopoly on the provision of learning opportunities, so the task of validating and certifying knowledge will also come to be distributed in much more free-form ways across networks of different types of provider. This would imply a radical departure from the current, centralised models of assessment towards something more closely resembling a marketplace, in which the regulator, the exam boards, or perhaps even local schools would act as 'brokers' for award structures designed by others.

Implications

This set of principles clearly has profound implications for the way we think about assessment and for the education system more widely. We consider here what we believe to be the five most important implications:

○   for **teachers' professional development** and the organisations that support it
○   for the **basic methods** used in assessment

- for **employers** and their interface with the assessment and qualifications system
- for the way **higher education** relates to school assessment
- for the relationship between assessment data and **performance management**

Teachers' professional development

Of course, to expect teachers to take up radically new assessment practices spontaneously is unrealistic, particularly since they may lack training beyond conventional methods for assessing their students' understandings. As one practitioner put it,[100] 'you can't take away the fact that teachers are accountable; they want to go with something they feel safe with'. In addition, opinion is sharply divided on how reliable teacher assessments are, although, as Paul Black has argued,[101] only a tiny fraction of the amount being spent on formal external examinations is being spent on research into how teacher assessments can be made more reliable.

What we need is to *broaden* the professional learning community around assessment for learning, by drawing in a much larger pool of teaching practitioners and academic researchers, and to *strengthen* it, by building more effective ways of sharing and creating knowledge about good practice. The building blocks of this professional learning community are already in place: the Assessment Reform Group is the nucleus of a research and development community that, as David Hargreaves argues, 'is in an international lead in advancing the theory and practice of formative assessment or assessment for learning. We must surely capitalise upon that lead.'[102] The National College for School Leadership's *Networked Learning Communities* initiative[103] should also generate a rich seam of useful knowledge. Here, clusters of schools receive funding and support in return for agreeing to a coordinated programme of enquiry-based improvement activities around a particular learning focus. A number of networks have decided to focus on assessment for learning. This points to an important and immediate challenge for policy-makers in **aligning the ongoing reform of the teaching workforce and school** organisation with the work of the task force on 14–19 reform now headed by Mike Tomlinson. The school reform agenda now contains several simultaneous strands of ongoing structural, organisational and policy change. The DfES has already initiated a review of assessment for learning practices and their potential to contribute to raising standards, and assessment for learning has become an explicit component of the Key Stage 3 strategy currently being implemented. The challenge facing policy-makers is to ensure that the further development of teachers' capacity to provide formative assessment on demand in reliable ways is developed in tandem with the wider restructuring of school-based provision and the creation of innovation and collaboration networks across schools and other providers.

Basic methods

Squaring the circle of improving both the validity of assessment and its reliability is a pressing challenge for researchers and practitioners alike. But the solution will almost certainly lie in diversifying the methods by which assessment is conducted. Team-based projects and exercises, computer simulations, presentations and orals, hands-on experiments and so on could help to make assessment more authentic, by widening the range of skills and competences that a learner can demonstrate, and so potentially make the inferences drawn from it more valid. In the interests of reliability, it would be important that these kinds of assessment take place more frequently, and less intrusively, than a conventional timed paper-and-pencil test. For this reason, they would generally need to be conducted in a classroom.

A central principle of reform in the qualifications system should therefore be that the system itself should be able to draw on a wider range of tools, techniques and methods of assessment, and that these can be incorporated into award structures progressively over time as their benefits and limitations in relation to other forms of assessment become clear.

Potentially, the key lubricant in enabling different methods of assessment to flow seamlessly into an overall assessment package is information and communication technology. ICTs have already had a major impact on the operation of assessment, in terms of processing, aggregation and analysis. Yet ICTs are rarely used for conducting assessment and identifying dimensions of learning performance, and it is here that it has the greatest potential impact. ICTs enable the information generated by assessment to be used in a wider range of contexts than existing formats. 'Digital portfolios' would enable assessment to become genuinely multifunctional, allowing a much greater range and volume of data to be held about learners in a more flexible, accessible and reusable format than paper.[104] The eVIVA electronic portfolio currently being piloted by Ultralab at Anglia Polytechnic University, with support from the QCA, offers an interesting platform on which to build. The bigger question, however, is how an integrated ICT-based portfolio of learning, potentially available to every learner, can be embedded in the evolution of new patterns of school organisation and the administration of qualifications in ways that enable a wider range of assessment tools and techniques.

Digital technologies open up the possibility of involving a much wider range of experts in validation of a performance, since performances can be recorded and viewed at distance. ICTs also make it possible for 'concept mapping',[105] and other group-based exercises for representing knowledge, to serve the purpose of assessing teamwork and collaborative skills by making it much easier to track the contribution of different members of a group.

Employers

The 14–19 Strategy makes involvement of employers a priority, not least because it envisages an expansion of work-related and work-based learning. But recent analysis of modern apprenticeships suggests that the current arrangements for developing collaborations between employers and awarding bodies are not fostering innovation. One illustration of this is the fact that the vast majority of employers are now aware of the Modern Apprenticeships programme, but that less than 15 per cent are directly involved in providing them. A new system, which seeks to maximise the choices, routes and modes of assessment available to learners about how they develop and validate work-based knowledge and skills, therefore, has to find new ways of binding in employers.

There are a range of ways in which this could be done:

○ New forms of incentive for employers to offer work-based learning, alongside more flexible systems for capturing this learning. Awarding bodies would play an enabling role, working with employers to develop awards that are bespoke to the needs of the company, but that are interoperable and therefore have an external value to those that achieve them.

○ New ways of involving employers in providing assessment services and standards. If we want assessment information about learners' performance in vocational contexts to be valid, it is clear that employers themselves must play a much more direct role in certifying their attainment. This already happens in some vocational courses, such as BTEC.

○ New local networks and partnerships between employers and learning providers. In Huddersfield, a leading design company based in the area has worked with the University of Huddersfield to develop a customised masters programme combining work-based and classroom learning. There is no reason why similar arrangements could not be pioneered between schools and local organisations in the private, public and voluntary sectors.

This kind of direct involvement can usefully be pioneered by the networks of interested organisations in various local settings: schools, colleges, Education–Business Partnerships, LEAs, Learning and Skills Councils, and so on. But to secure the meaningful engagement of employers across the country, central government will also need to make this an explicit priority. In doing so, it should also make direct connections with the national infrastructure now being established to support a demand-led system of adult learning and skills development.

Higher education

For decades, higher education has kept the assessment and qualifications system in a kind of stranglehold; universities must occupy a pivotal place in the creation of a new system. In particular, the sector will have to change radically both the kinds of information that they use to allocate places, and the systems they put in place to collect this information.

The key to establishing the place of universities in the process of reinvention is to understand the multiple roles that they might perform:

○   as experts on certain kinds of disciplinary knowledge, and the thinking skills that underpin them
○   as a major influence on the type of assessment information that schools and others take seriously
○   as a source of demand for certain kinds of learning ability, particularly around basic skills, study methods and the learning to learn skills.

Accepting that the current points system is increasingly unsustainable, not least because it is harder and harder to differentiate between students, and that a reshaped system would not prioritise assessment information of the kind currently used to sort and rank students, two possibilities emerge.

The first is that universities embrace a model of standardised, cognitive ability testing along the lines of the American SAT. Given the wider arguments we have made in this pamphlet, it should be no surprise to learn that this is not an approach we would endorse. Although there might be some role for cognitive testing within a wider repertoire of methods, anything approaching a reliance on such tests would be a catastrophic mistake. It would recreate and reinforce many of the problems with the validity of existing assessments, and have a highly distortionary impact on the operation of the school system more widely.

The second is that universities engineer a shift away from the points system and take the lead in developing new, portfolio-based systems that draw on many different types of information. Using their disciplinary expertise, they would work to build rich and detailed profiles of the kind of learners they want to select for different courses. By prioritising depth of understanding and ability to learn in recruiting students, they could actively transcend some of the debates and controversies that have developed over access and selection, by being able to base their decisions on a much more sophisticated understanding of what different learners are capable of than the standard information currently provides.

Performance management

The use of summative pupil data to evaluate the performance of schools and colleges has become a fundamental part of the system. For all its inadequacies, this provides a very clear means of evaluating the performance of a particular age cohort as it progresses through the school system, and comparing it with similar groups in other schools or areas. But if we take as our starting point that assessment will be undertaken with future learning progress as its first priority, and that other uses will not undermine that purpose, then it is clear that these kinds of metrics and instruments would need to be recast.

The bedrock of a new approach would be a form of moderated teacher assessment, but employed in a very different context from the way that it has been traditionally. In particular, the role of the teacher would be reshaped around the delivery of assessment for learning in the classroom. Instead of the routine aggregation of all summative pupil data, this would be coupled with a much more sophisticated approach for transforming this formative assessment data into performance information about schools and teachers. This is certainly not beyond the capability of schools. One option would be the system of 'light-sampling' proposed by Wiliam,[106] whereby every student in a class would be randomly assigned a particular assessment task. Although unreliable in terms of the individual pupil, this would be very reliable in terms of the overall performance of the class. There would also be no incentive for teachers to narrow their focus, since everything on the syllabus could be expected to come up.

Once the implications of assessment on demand begin to filter through, the performance management infrastructure of standardised scores and league tables would need to be recast to capture and reflect much more strongly the distance travelled by learners, and the value added by schools, as the key metrics of success.

Unanswered questions

The trade-off in trying to focus attention on the broad principles of reform is that some key questions remain unanswered. In particular, the question of educational entitlement – itself beginning to emerge half-formed within the mainstream debate – is brought into sharp relief by the analysis presented above. A system of personalised, pathway-driven progression based on assessment on demand does not sit comfortably with an age-based concept of educational entitlement. The Learning Licence would provide one way of framing the 'offer' made to learners as citizens: that each is entitled to become qualified to learn. But that would force us to make quite explicit our beliefs about the nature of human potential. Should learners be given as long as they need to reach this level of competency? Or is it unrealistic to expect even the most personalised of systems to enable every learner to reach this standard? This in turn raises the question of funding. Although measures to make funding follow the learner not the institution are beginning to be experimented with, we are a long way from the model of lifelong learning funding that would best support personalisation and flexibility in what entitlement meant from one learner to another.

The reason for staying silent on this, and the myriad other questions that the wider analysis provokes, is twofold. In the first instance, there is the problem of overload. It would be very easy for this approach to turn into a grand theory of everything, especially when the assessment system is bound up and intertwined with so many other dimensions of education policy. But the second, and more important, point is that the way to answer these questions is not to offer a definitive solution in a pamphlet but to create the conditions in which they might emerge through practice, experimentation and learning.

This brings us back to the nature of scientific revolutions and the question of how they are, and are not, precipitated. It is worth reflecting for a moment on this question, and its implications for policy-making.

A new paradigm is not introduced from the top of hierarchies and rolled out according to some rationalistic plan or 'change management' strategy. Instead it emerges, incoherently at first, from practices at various locations across the system. It starts to take shape when there is enough room for manoeuvre in the system to allow these practices to flourish and replicate. It becomes dominant when enough people realise that it represents a more authentic and powerful way of capturing the essence of what they are trying to do or to understand, and when organisational and institutional arrangements have adapted far enough to make it possible to scale up and apply these new ideas across the whole system.

In assessment, we are perhaps only at the beginning of that process. We have reached the point where dissatisfaction with our current modes of assessment could make it possible for radical alternatives to emerge, and where many different stakeholders could be involved in helping to create something radically different. But as yet there is no focus around which these dissenting voices can begin to cohere, because the current political and regulatory climate is configured to encourage conformity not diversity, and compliance not creativity. These design constraints are very real. Yet it is only by stepping outside the parameters of the current system, and imagining and articulating the part that assessment might play in a totally different approach to learning and the certification of knowledge, that we can stimulate the deviance on which long-term renewal depends.

Conclusion: the perils of the gold standard

In this report, we have drawn together compelling evidence of the need for radical reform of our assessment and qualifications system. We have argued that the existing system is labouring under a heavy burden of competing expectations and logistical complexity. It has survived only at the expense of its overall fitness-for-purpose.

But however compelling the case for change, and however powerful the intellectual, social, economic or technological forces providing the impetus for it, the contests about how the system should adapt have long been, and will remain, fundamentally *political.*

Despite the rhetorical commitment, from all sides, to widening participation in education and the genuinely shared consensus that investment in learning and skills is essential to both a competitive economy and a vibrant society, we still seem unable to let go of the idea that assessment is primarily a 'funnel' for selecting the most able.

In 1988, the Higginson Report recommended wholesale reform of the structure of A-levels, but it was quickly rejected by Prime Minister Margaret Thatcher. The A-level, she said, was the 'gold standard': effective, widely respected, and untouchable. Her choice of metaphor is ironic. In the 1920s, a similarly dogmatic commitment to the original 'gold standard' had resulted in an unsustainable and ultimately disastrous monetary policy. In both cases, the political imperative was to follow the prevailing orthodoxy and preserve the status quo, despite overwhelming evidence of the risks of doing so. How long before we realise that to cling on to what worked in the past will not provide us with the assessment system we need for the future?

Appendix 1 Demos/Edexcel Symposium

On 28 June 2002, Demos and Edexcel hosted a one-day symposium on the future of educational assessment at the Commonwealth Club in London. 'Measuring People or Measuring Schools?' brought together 50 experts and practitioners for a series of plenary discussions and workshops. The ideas that came out of the symposium have been very helpful in informing and shaping this pamphlet, and we are grateful to all those attended, particularly those who presented or responded to papers: Professors Wynne Harlen, Patricia Broadfoot (both University of Bristol) and Paul Black (King's College, London), Tim Cornford (NfER/Nelson Publishing), John Kerr (Edexcel), David Hawker (Brighton and Hove Council), Tony Mackay (Centre for Strategic Educational Thinking) and Riel Miller (OECD).

Appendix 2 Methodological note

The research has been eclectic in its selection of evidence bases. The overarching theoretical narrative has been provided by systems thinking, which conceives of major public services like education as 'complex adaptive systems', and is well suited to understanding the challenges of managing and reforming an enterprise of the complexity of the assessment and qualifications system (see Appendix 5, below).

However, we have also drawn more detailed insights from the latest research on the theory of learning,[107] recent international evidence on comparative educational performance,[108] a growing body of work on the theory and practice of 'assessment for learning',[109] a major study of the impact of assessment on learners' motivation,[110] and literature on various aspects of the information society.[111] It has also been informed by interviews with practitioners and experts, and by the discussions at a Demos/Edexcel Symposium on the future of assessment (see Appendix 1).

Although it is specifically grounded in the experience of the English assessment system, the pamphlet deals with issues and challenges that are common to a wide range of assessment and qualifications systems, and much of its analysis will be relevant and applicable across territorial boundaries. More importantly, it is also hoped that in terms of both the analysis of the problems facing the assessment and qualifications system and the character of our recommendations for solving them, this pamphlet will provide some wider lessons for government and other stakeholders about the nature of whole system change *per se*. To what extent and by what means complex, large-scale enterprises can develop a self-sustaining capacity for adaptation and renewal is a crucial question whose importance extends far beyond the functional and institutional parameters of the assessment and qualifications system.

Appendix 3   Structure of the assessment regime

The assessment regime has undergone major restructuring in recent years. A series of mergers between smaller exam boards has led to the creation of just three 'unitary awarding bodies' for England:

○   The Assessment and Qualifications Alliance (**AQA**) was formed in October 1998 by the merger of the Associated Examining Board (AEB), Southern Examining Group (SEG) and the Northern Examinations and Assessment Board (NEAB).

○   **Edexcel** was created in 1996 with the merger of the Awarding Body of the University of London Examinations and Assessment Council (ULEAC) and BTEC, one of the principal providers of vocational qualifications.

○   Oxford, Cambridge and RSA (or **OCR** for short) incorporates the Midland Examining Group (MEG), Oxford and Cambridge Examinations and Assessment Council (OCEAC) and the RSA Examinations Board. It was established in October 1998.

This restructuring has been mirrored by evolving integration at the regulatory level:

○   The 1993 Dearing Report recommended that the National Curriculum Council (NCC) and Schools Examination and Assessment Council (SEAC) be merged in one body: the School Curriculum and Assessment Authority (SCAA). This was enacted in the 1993 Education Act.

○   The 1997 Education Act sought to bring together the regulation of academic and vocational qualifications in one body through the merger of the SCAA with the National Council for Vocational Qualifications (NCVQ). The new body became the Qualifications Curriculum Authority, or QCA.

The exam boards are both limited companies and charities. They are accredited by QCA to offer qualifications, and QCA reserves the right to withdraw this accreditation either for the organisation as a whole, or for individual qualifications.

Appendix 4 The PISA study

The Programme for International Student Assessment (PISA) is a collaborative effort among the member countries of the OECD to measure how well young adults, at age 15 and approaching the end of compulsory schooling, are prepared to meet the challenges of contemporary society.

PISA assesses students across three 'domains' of literacy: scientific literacy, reading literacy and mathematical literacy. The domains were broken down in terms of:

○   the **content** or structure of knowledge that students need to acquire
○   the **processes** that need to be performed
○   the **contexts** in which knowledge and skills are applied.

The term 'literacy' was used to denote a broader conception of attainment than that usually captured in assessment, with an emphasis on students' capacity to apply knowledge and skills to real-life situations rather than on the extent to which they have mastered a specific curriculum.

The first assessment (focusing on reading literacy) is being completed for 2000–2. It will be repeated on a three-year cycle, with the focus on mathematics in 2003, science in 2006 and back to reading in 2009.

For more information, see OECD.[112]

Appendix 5 Systems thinking

Systems thinking is a way of looking at the world that emphasises the importance of taking a holistic view of how things fit together, looking at how different elements join together to form *complex* wholes: systems. It is built on the concept of 'emergent properties': put simply, the idea that the whole is greater than the sum of its parts. It contends that it is not just the individual components of a system but the nature of the interactions and interconnections between them which matter.[113] Instead of trying to solve complex problems by breaking them up into smaller, more manageable but discrete chunks, it goes up a level of abstraction to develop solutions that try to improve the performance of the system as a whole.

As well as being complex, systems can be described as *adaptive*, in that they have the capacity to withstand often quite fundamental changes in their external environment by changing some aspects of their behaviour. Understanding what changes and what is preserved when a complex adaptive system is forced to adapt to a major change in its environment is crucial to the challenge of reform. More often than not the adaptive response amounts to superficial reordering of institutional structures, while what is conserved is a more fundamental set of values, mindsets and assumptions about 'the way things work'. Finding ways to change the latter is essential if the system is to perform in a more desirable way, but to succeed changes must grow from within the system, and not be imposed on it from without.

In thinking about public policy problems it is useful to differentiate between 'messes' and 'difficulties'. Difficult problems are those to which a solution can be found because there is a broad agreement on what the problem is and what the solution should look like. Other problems are very clearly policy 'messes', characterised by no clear agreement about what the problem is, what the process of improvement might look like, or what the time and resources needed to understand and solve it might be. While rational analysis may yield the answer to a difficult problem, when applied to a messy problem it will simply generate modes of failure like those described above. Systems thinking, on the other hand, is well suited to tackling messy problems because 'it recognises and works with the ambiguity inherent in a situation'.[114]

Finally, the absence of a single 'right answer' to messy problems is largely because all stakeholders interpret the world through the lens of their own differing values and experiences. A recognition of the existence – and the validity – of *multiple perspectives* or 'frames' on an issue is a central feature of systems thinking and practice.

For a more detailed introduction to systems thinking, see the Demos pamphlet *System Failure* by Jake Chapman.

References and links

1 J Bransford, A Brown and R Cocking (eds), *How People Learn: brain, mind, experience and school* (Washington, DC: National Academy Press, 2000).

2 M Castells, *The Rise of the Network Society*, 2nd edn (Oxford: Blackwells, 2000).

3 D Mercer, 'The future of education in Europe until 2010', *Demographic and Social Trends Issue Paper No. 6* (European Commission JRC: EUR 18968 EN, 1999). Available at: ftp://ftp.jrc.es/pub/EURdoc/eur18968en.pdf.

4 eg AS/A2 levels, VCE (vocational A-level), BTEC, NVQ Level 3 or Advanced Modern Apprenticeships.

5 National Skills Task Force, *Skills for All: proposals for a national skills agenda*, Final Report of the NSTF (London: DfEE, 2000). Available at: www.dfee.gov.uk/skillsforce/skillsforall.pdf.

6 ie the amount of time it takes for their value to halve.

7 OECD, *Human Capital Investment: an international comparison* (Paris: OECD, 1998).

8 P Black, C Harrison, C Lee et al, *Working inside the Black Box* (London: KCL, 2002).

9 R Heifetz, *Leadership Without Easy Answers* (London: Belknap Press, 1994).

10 Department for Education and Skills, *14–19: Opportunity and excellence* (London: DfES, 2003).

11 D Schön, *Beyond the Stable State* (London: Temple Smith, 1971).

12 D Wiliam, *Technical Issues in the Development and Implementation of a System of Criterion-referenced Age-independent Levels of Attainment in the National Curriculum of England and Wales* (London: KCL, 1993). Wiliam marshals evidence that teachers can predict which aspects of a subject will be tested.

13 A Chrisafis, 'Widespread cheating devalues school tests', *Guardian*, 28 October 2002.

14 E Baker, B McGaw and Lord Sutherland, *Maintaining GCE A-Level Standards: the findings of an independent panel of experts* (2002). Available at: www.internationalpanel.org.uk.

15 R Smithers, 'Exam regulator ordered to make urgent reforms', *Guardian*, 18 June 2002. Available at: www.guardian.co.uk/uk_news/story/0,3604,739399,00.html.

16 This concept is discussed in J Cubbin and D Currie, *Regulatory Creep and Regulatory Withdrawal: why regulatory withdrawal is feasible and necessary* (London: City University Business School, 2002).

17 M Tomlinson, *Inquiry into A level Standards*, Interim Report, 2002. Available at: www.dfes.gov.uk/docs/alevel-interim-report.htm.

18 See, for example, R Smithers, 'A-level student sues for £100,000 over "grade fixing"', *Guardian*, 7 October 2002.

19 J Chapman, *System Failure: why governments must learn to think differently* (London: Demos, 2002).

20 Task Group on Assessment and Testing, *National Curriculum Task Group on Assessment and Testing: a report* (London: Department of Education and Science, 1988).

21 D Hargreaves, 'Assessing assessment', OCR/KPMG lecture at the RSA,

London, 13 February 2002. Available at: www.rsa.org.uk/acrobat/hargreaves_13feb02.pdf.

22 J Biggs, 'Enhancing teaching through constructive alignment', *Higher Education*, 32(3) (1996): 347–64.

23 Ibid.

24 J Biggs, 'Enhancing teaching through constructive alignment'; and R Rothman, J Slattery, J Vranek, and L Resnick, *Benchmarking and Alignment of Standards and Testing*, CSE Technical Report 566 (Los Angeles, CA: CRESST, 2002). Available at: http://cresst96.cse.ucla.edu/CRESST/Reports/TR566.pdf.

25 Central Statistical Office, *Social Trends No 22: 1992 edition* (London: HMSO, 1992); Department for Education and Skills, *Participation in Education, Training and Employment by 16–18 year olds in England: 2000 and 2001*, SFR 16/2002 (London: DfES, 2002). Available at: www.dfes.gov.uk/statistics/DB/SFR/s0341/sfr16-2002.pdf; and Office for National Statistics, *Social Trends No 30: 2000 edition* (London: The Stationery Office, 2000).

26 Office for National Statistics, *Social Trends No 30*.

27 Office for National Statistics, *Social Trends No 32: 2002 edition* (London: The Stationery Office, 2002). Available at: www.nationalstatistics.gov.uk/downloads/theme_social/Social_Trends32/Social_Trends32.pdf.

28 Department for Education and Skills, *14–19: Extending opportunities, raising standards*, Summary (London: DfES, 2002b). Available at: www.dfes.gov.uk/14-

19greenpaper/download/GreenPaperSummary.pdf.

29 DfES, *14–19: Opportunity and excellence*.

30 DfES, *14–19: Extending opportunities, raising standards*.

31 Joint Council for General Qualifications, *Media Brief, Summer 2002*, 2002. Available at: www.jcgq.org.uk/Media_and_center/Media_Brief_2002.PDF.

32 Professional Association of Teachers, *Tested to Destruction?: a survey of examination stress in teenagers* (Derby: PAT, 2002).

33 R Smithers, 'More exams + high costs = failure', *Guardian*, 23 January 2002. Available at: http://education.guardian.co.uk/aslevels/story/0,10495,637894,00.html.

34 W Woodward, 'Exams watchdog seeks tests cutback', *Guardian*, 2 December 2002.

35 P Black and D Wiliam, *Inside the Black Box* (London: KCL, 1998). An abridged version is available at: www.kcl.ac.uk/depsta/education/publications/blackbox.html. In fact, as Black and Wiliam argue, teachers' contributions to summative assessments have been very marginal.

36 eg Department of Education and Science, *The National Curriculum 5–16 – a consultation* (London: Department for Education and Science, 1987).

37 Department of Education and Science, *Advancing A Levels. The Higginson Report* (London: HMSO, 1988).

38 A more detailed explanation of the new AS/A2 system is provided by the QCA. See: www.qca.org.uk/nq/framework/framework3.asp.

39 Qualifications and Curriculum

Authority, *Review of Curriculum 2000 – QCA's report on phase one* (London: QCA, 2001). Available at: www.qca.org.uk/nq/framework/advice.pdf; and Qualifications and Curriculum Authority, *Review of Curriculum 2000 – QCA's report on phase two* (London: QCA, 2001). Available at: www.qca.org.uk/nq/framework/c2k/c2k_phase2.pdf.

40 Tomlinson, *Inquiry into A level Standards*, Interim Report.

41 For a more detailed history, see Appendix 3.

42 Qualifications and Curriculum Authority, *Quinquennial Review* (London: QCA, 2002). Available at: www.qca.org.uk/pdf.asp?/about/quinquennial_review.pdf. A more negative interpretation is offered by Lowe, who presents an interesting case for how the globalisation of qualifications represents a form of 'credentialism' designed to disadvantage people from developing countries in the competition for access to the most advantageous labour market opportunities. See: J Lowe, 'International examinations: the new credentialism and reproduction of advantage in a globalising world', *Assessment in Education*, 7(3) (2000): 363–77.

43 O O'Neill, 'Called to Account', *The Reith Lectures* 2002, Number 3. Available at: www.bbc.co.uk/radio4/reith2002/lecture3_text.shtml.

44 M Tomlinson, *Inquiry into A level Standards*, Final Report, 2002. Available at: www.dfes.gov.uk/alevelsinquiry/.

45 Baker et al, *Maintaining GCE A-Level Standards*.

46 R Smithers, 'Exam regulator ordered to make urgent reforms'.

47 D Wiliam, 'The meanings and consequences of educational assessments', *Critical Quarterly*, 42(1) (2000): 105–27.

48 D Wiliam, 'An overview of the relationship between assessment and the curriculum' in D Scott (ed), *Curriculum and Assessment* (Greenwich, CT: JAI Press, 2001); and Tomlinson, *Inquiry into A level Standards*, Final Report.

49 Tomlinson, *Inquiry into A level Standards*, Final Report.

50 Department for Education and Skills, *The Future of Higher Education* (London: DfES, 2003).

51 P Black and D Wiliam, *Standards in Public Examinations* (London: KCL, 2002).

52 Estelle Morris, quoted in R Smithers, 'Exam regulator ordered to make urgent reforms'.

53 P Senge, *The Fifth Discipline: the art and practice of the learning organization* (New York: Doubleday, 1990).

54 M Chassin, 'Is health care ready for six sigma quality?', *The Millbank Quarterly*, 76(4) (1998): 565–91.

55 P Senge, *The Fifth Discipline*.

56 L Shepard, *The Role of Classroom Assessment in Teaching and Learning*, CSE Technical Report 517 (Los Angeles, CA: Center for the Study of Evaluation, 2000). Available at: http://cresst96.cse.ucla.edu/CRESST/Reports/TECH517.pdf.

57 ie where there is a lot riding on the outcome of that *particular* assessment, whether for the learner, teacher or school.

58 G Delandshere, 'Implicit theories, unexamined assumptions and the status quo of educational assessment', *Assessment in Education*, 8(2) (2001): 113–33.

59   Black and Wiliam, *Standards in Public Examinations*.
60   Ibid.
61   Bransford et al, *How People Learn*.
62   R Glaser and P Baxter, *Assessing Active Knowledge*, CSE Technical Report 516 (Los Angeles, CA: CRESST, 2000). Available at: http://cresst96.cse.ucla.edu/ CRESST/Reports/TECH516.PDF.
63   Wiliam, 'An overview of the relationship between assessment and the curriculum'.
64   L Resnick and D Resnick, 'Assessing the thinking curriculum: new tools for educational reform', in B Gifford and M O'Connor (eds), *Changing Assessments: alternative views of aptitude, achievement and instruction* (Boston, MA: Kluwer, 1992).
65   Linn and Baker, cited in D Wiliam, 'National curriculum assessment: how to make it better', *Research Papers in Education* 2003 (in press).
66   D Wiliam, *Level Best? Levels of Attainment in National Curriculum Assessment* (London: ATL, 2001).
67   Linn, cited in D Wiliam, 'Integrating formative and summative functions of assessment', paper presented to Working Group 10 of the International Congress on Mathematics Education, Makuhari, Tokyo, August 2000.
68   Association of Teachers and Lecturers, *An Evaluation of the 1999 Key Stage 3 Tests in English, Mathematics and Science* (London: ATL, 1999).
69   Chapman, *System Failure*.
70   Black and Wiliam, *Standards in Public Examinations*.
71   Tomlinson, *Inquiry into A level Standards*, Final Report.
72   D Rogasa, *Accuracy of Individual Scores Expressed in Percentile Ranks: classical test theory calculations* (Los Angeles, CA: CRESST, 1999). Available at: www.cse.ucla.edu/CRESST/Reports/ TECH509.PDF.
73   D Rogasa, *Accuracy of Individual Scores Expressed in Percentile Ranks*; Wiliam, 'National curriculum assessment: how to make it better'; and Black and Wiliam, *Standards in Public Examinations*.
74   Wiliam, 'The meanings and consequences of educational assessments'.
75   Wiliam, 'Integrating formative and summative functions of assessment'; and Wiliam, 'The meanings and consequences of educational assessments'.
76   G Orwell, *Animal Farm* (Harmondsworth: Penguin, 1951).
77   W Harlen and R Deakin-Crick, *A Systematic Review of the Impact of Summative Assessment and Tests on Students' Motivation for Learning* (London: EPPI-Centre, 2002). Available at: http://eppi.ioe.ac.uk/ EPPIWeb/home.aspx?page=/reel/ review_groups/assessment/ review_one.htm.
78   Black and Wiliam, *Inside the Black Box*.
79   Harlen and Deakin-Crick, *A Systematic Review of the Impact of Summative Assessment and Tests on Students' Motivation for Learning*.
80   Ibid.
81   E Goddard and V Higgins, *Smoking, Drinking and Drug Use Amongst Teenagers in 1998* (London: The Stationery Office, 1999).
82   P Senge, N Cambron-McCabe, T Lucas et al, *Schools That Learn* (London: Nicholas Brealey, 2000).

83 T Kuhn, *The Structure of Scientific Revolutions* (Chicago: University of Chicago Press, 1970).

84 Bransford et al, *How People Learn*.

85 For a more detailed exposition, see Shepard, *The Role of Classroom Assessment in Teaching and Learning* and Bransford et al, *How People Learn*.

86 Shepard, *The Role of Classroom Assessment in Teaching and Learning*.

87 Bransford et al, *How People Learn*.

88 Ibid.

89 Ibid.

90 Ibid.

91 Ibid.

92 H Gardner, *The Disciplined Mind* (New York: Simon & Schuster, 1999).

93 Glaser and Baxter, *Assessing Active Knowledge*.

94 Assessment Reform Group, *Assessment for Learning: 10 principles* (2002). Available at: www.assessment-reform-group.org.uk.

95 Ibid.

96 Bransford et al, *How People Learn*.

97 Black and Wiliam, *Inside the Black Box*.

98 Ibid.

99 Gardner, *The Disciplined Mind*.

100 Contribution to the Demos/Edexcel Symposium.

101 Ibid.

102 Hargreaves, 'Assessing assessment'.

103 For more information, see www.ncsl.org.uk/nlc.

104 R Jupp, T Bentley and C Fairley, *What Learning Needs: the challenge for a creative nation* (London: Demos, 2001).

105 E Plotnick, 'Concept mapping: a graphical system for understanding the relationship between concepts', (Syracuse, NY: ERIC Clearinghouse on Information & Technology, 1997). Available at: http://ericit.org/digests/EDO-IR-1997-05.shtml.

106 Wiliam, 'An overview of the relationship between assessment and the curriculum'.

107 eg Bransford et al, *How People Learn*.

108 OECD, *Knowledge and Skills for Life: first results from PISA 2000* (Paris: OECD, 2001).

109 Black and Wiliam, *Inside the Black Box*.

110 Harlen and Deakin-Crick, *A Systematic Review of the Impact of Summative Assessment and Tests on Students' Motivation for Learning*.

111 eg Castells, *The Rise of the Network Society*; and OECD, *Measuring What People Know: human capital accounting for the knowledge economy* (Paris: OECD, 1996).

112 OECD, *Knowledge and Skills for Life*.

113 Chapman, *System Failure*.

114 Ibid.